Complete EnglishSmart

REVISED AND UPDATED!

2

D1501499

Complete EnglishSmart Contents

The Bumblebee

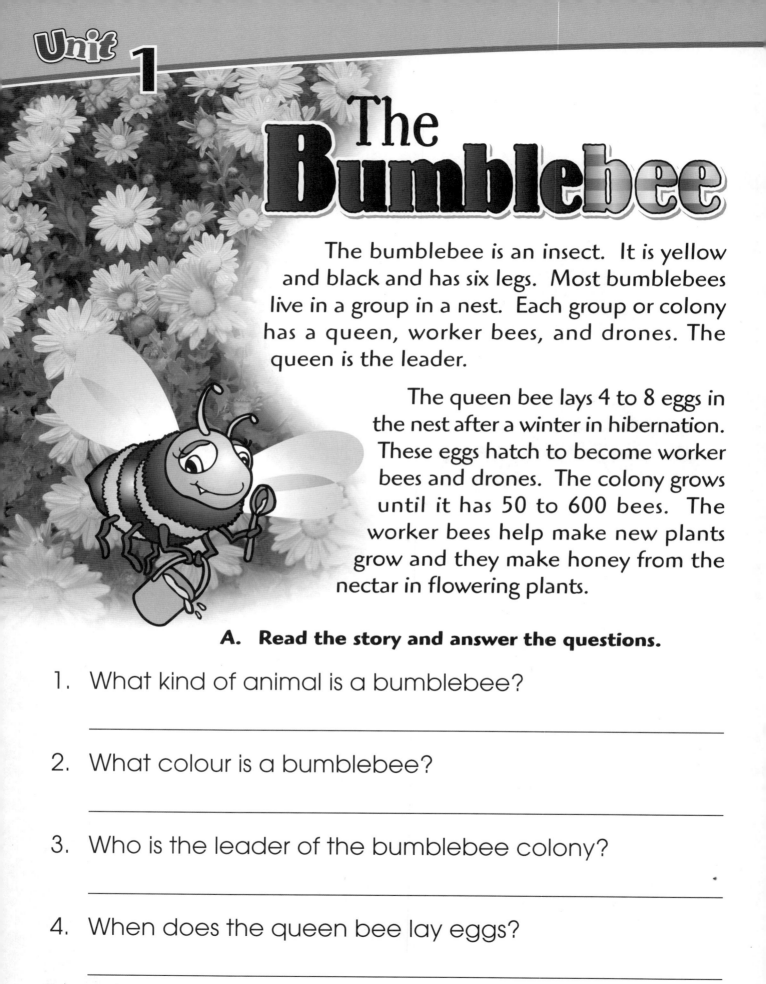

The bumblebee is an insect. It is yellow and black and has six legs. Most bumblebees live in a group in a nest. Each group or colony has a queen, worker bees, and drones. The queen is the leader.

The queen bee lays 4 to 8 eggs in the nest after a winter in hibernation. These eggs hatch to become worker bees and drones. The colony grows until it has 50 to 600 bees. The worker bees help make new plants grow and they make honey from the nectar in flowering plants.

A. Read the story and answer the questions.

1. What kind of animal is a bumblebee?

   _____

2. What colour is a bumblebee?

   _____

3. Who is the leader of the bumblebee colony?

   _____

4. When does the queen bee lay eggs?

   _____

Phonics: Beginning Consonants

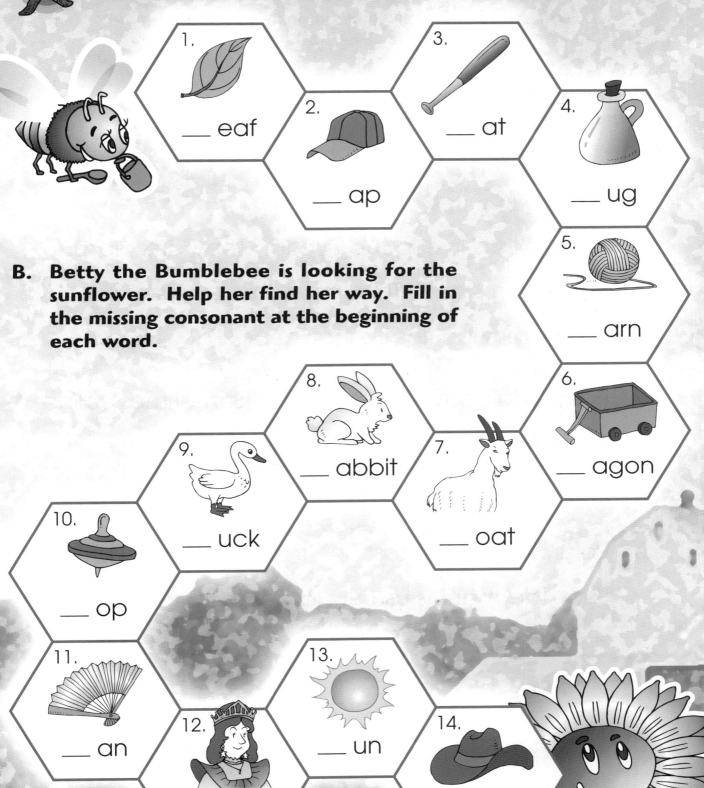

1. __ eaf

2. __ ap

3. __ at

4. __ ug

B. Betty the Bumblebee is looking for the sunflower. Help her find her way. Fill in the missing consonant at the beginning of each word.

5. __ arn

6. __ agon

7. __ oat

8. __ abbit

9. __ uck

10. __ op

11. __ an

12. __ ueen

13. __ un

14. __ at

 Sentence Recognition

- A **Sentence** is a group of words that tells a complete thought about someone or something.

C. Underline the groups of words that are not complete sentences.

1. Polar bears live in the Arctic. They are big and white. Big paws. They have small eyes and ears. Jump from ice floe to ice floe.

2. Polar bears have other names. Sometimes called white bears, sea bears, or ice bears. Swim very well.

3. Polar bears move fast and travel far. Eat seals and fish. The male is usually larger than the female. Hairy feet.

4. Baby bears or cubs are born in winter. Weigh 2 pounds when born. Remain with mothers from 10 months to 2 years.

Code Word Game

D.   Help Tim use the code below to read the sentences.

A	B	C	D	E	F	G	H	I	J	K	L	M	N	O
1	2	3	4	5	6	7	8	9	10	11	12	13	14	15

P	Q	R	S	T	U	V	W	X	Y	Z
16	17	18	19	20	21	22	23	24	25	26

1.

___ ___ ___ ___ ___ ___ ___
1   19 17 21 1   18 5

___ ___ ___ ___ ___ ___ ___ ___
9   19 1   19 8   1   16 5

___ ___ ___ ___ ___ ___ ___ ___
23 9   20 8   6   15 21 18

___ ___ ___ ___ ___
5   17 21 1   12

___ ___ ___ ___ ___ .
19 9   4   5   19

2.

___ ___ ___ ___ ___ ___ ___ ___ ___
1   20 18 9   1   14 7   12 5

___ ___ ___ ___ ___ ___ ___ ___
9   19 1   19 8   1   16 5

___ ___ ___ ___ ___ ___ ___ ___ ___
23 9   20 8   20 8   18 5   5

___ ___ ___ ___ ___ .
19 9   4   5   19

3.

___ ___ ___ ___ ___ ___ ___
1   3   9   18 3   12 5

___ ___ ___ ___ ___ ___ ___ ___ ___
9   19 1   19 9   14 7   12 5

___ ___ ___ ___ .
12 9   14 5

4.

___ ___ ___ ___ ___ ___ ___ ___ ___ ___
1   18 5   3   20 1   14 7   12 5

___ ___ ___ ___ ___ ___ ___ ___
9   19 1   19 8   1   16 5

___ ___ ___ ___
23 9   20 8

___ ___ ___ ___ ___ ___ ___ ___
15 16 16 15 19 9   20 5

___ ___ ___ ___ ___ ___ ___ ___ ___
19 9   4   5   19 20 8   1   20

___ ___ ___ ___ ___ ___ ___ ___ .
1   18 5   5   17 21 1   12

The Museum Trip

Tomorrow our class is going on a trip to the R.O.M. (Royal Ontario Museum). We will leave school at 9:00 a.m. and return at 3:00 p.m. We will have to take our lunch with us.

When we get to the museum, we will visit the Bat Cave, the dinosaurs, and the Egyptian mummies.

The day after our trip, when we get back to school, we will draw pictures and write about what we saw there.

ROM
Royal Ontario Museum

A. Circle the correct answers.

1. What is the story about?

   A. visiting the school   B. a trip to the museum
   C. looking at dinosaurs

2. What will the children take with them?

   A. snacks   B. lunch   C. a school bag

3. Which of these will they see?

   A. paintings   B. mummies   C. toys

4. What will they do after the trip?

   A. play a game B. watch a movie C. draw pictures

Phonics: Middle and Ending Consonants

B. Look at the pictures. Fill in the missing consonants.

1.  bu ___

2. 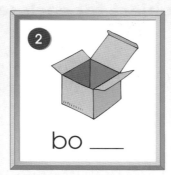 bo ___

3.  nes ___

4.  di ___ e

5.  tuli ___

6.  mas ___

7.  ba ___

8.  po ___

9. 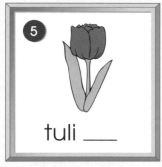 pe ___

10. 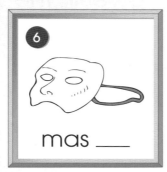 bo ___ e

11.  ca ___

12.  bal ___

13.  soc ___

14. 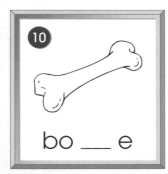 sa ___

15.  ki ___ e

16.  ra ___ e

 Subject of a Sentence

- The **Subject** part of a sentence tells whom or what the sentence is about.

C. Look at the pictures. Write a subject for each sentence.

1. _____ are my favourite fruit.

2. _____ is the tallest self-supporting tower in the world.

3. _____ rotates around the sun.

4. _____ has a monitor and a keyboard.

5. _____ is my favourite sport.

6. _____ is 8:15 a.m.

7. Draw and write.

_____ is what I like to do with friends.

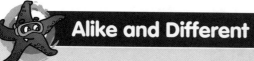

Alike and Different

- You can compare things by looking at how they are alike and how they are different. If two things are **alike**, something about them is the same. If two things are **different**, something about them is not the same.

D. Read the sentences. Put a check mark ✔ in the box to indicate the sport being described.

	Hockey	Baseball
1. We play it on ice.		
2. We play it on a field.		
3. Something is hit.		
4. There are goalposts.		
5. Players run.		
6. Players wear skates.		
7. Players wear caps.		
8. Scores are kept.		

The Eurotunnel

Have you heard of the Eurotunnel? It is the longest undersea tunnel in the world. We can travel from England to France through this tunnel.

The idea of a tunnel running under the English Channel is not new. As early as 1802, a French engineer tried to convince the emperor Napoleon to build one. In 1993, it was finally built.

The Eurotunnel actually consists of three tunnels: one for trains that carry people in one direction and another for trains to carry people in the opposite direction. A third service tunnel allows fresh air, repair workers, and emergency vehicles to reach the train tunnels.

A. Give short answers to the questions.

1. Which countries are linked by the Eurotunnel?

_____

2. When was the Eurotunnel built?

_____

3. Who was the French emperor in 1802?

   _____

4. Why are there three tunnels?

   _____

Phonics: Short Vowels

B. Rob is looking for the tunnel. Help him find his way. Fill in the missing vowels a, e, i, o, or u.

14. r __ ck

13. t __ nt

12. f __ n

1. l __ mp

15. s __ x

11. l __ ps

2. w __ b

16. n __ t

10. c __ n

3. m __ p

9. n __ t

4. j __ g

5. p __ t

6. b __ g

7. d __ sk

8. b __ ll

Predicate of a Sentence

- The **Predicate** is the part of the sentence that tells what the subject is doing.

C. Write a predicate for each sentence.

1. In spring, flowers _____
   _____ .

2. In summer, we _____
   _____ .

3. In fall, I _____
   _____ .

4. In winter, I _____
   _____ .

5. My favourite sport _____
   _____ .

6. On Mother's Day, we _____
   _____ .

7. In my dream, I _____
   _____ .

8. My family _____
   _____ .

Classification / Grouping

D. **Louise the Ladybug wants to sort some words. Write the words that belong to each group under the first word.**

cup   blackboard   desk   swing   eraser

seesaw   pear   bowl   slide   tires   horn

grapes   apple   glass   key

1. cupboard

_____

_____

2. school

_____

_____

3. car

_____

_____

4. playground

_____

_____

5. fruit

_____

_____

Snakes

A. Jake the Snake needs help to finish the story. Fill in the missing words for him.

Snakes are 1._____ that have 2._____ , slender bodies. They have no limbs. They are 3._____ -blooded because they have a low body temperature.

Snakes are non-mammals because they lay 4._____ , which hatch soon after they are 5._____ . They go into 6._____ , or a kind of sleep, for part of the year. Snakes shed their 7._____ several times a year. They 8._____ by slithering from one 9._____ to another.

cold   laid   long
eggs   reptiles
hibernation   move
skins   place

Phonics: Long Vowels

B. Help Jeff the Snake look for his friend. Fill in the blanks with **a, i, o,** or **u.**

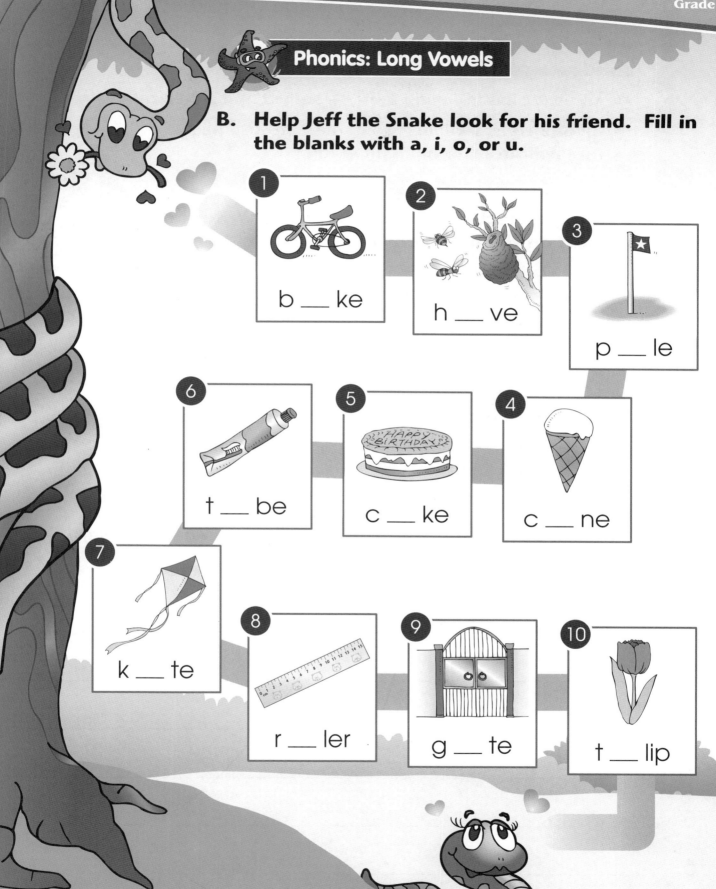

1. b __ ke

2. h __ ve

3. p __ le

6. t __ be

5. c __ ke

4. c __ ne

7. k __ te

8. r __ ler

9. g __ te

10. t __ lip

 Distinguishing Subjects and Predicates

- A sentence has two main parts – a **Subject** and a **Predicate**.
- The **Subject** tells whom or what the sentence is about.
- The **Predicate** tells what is happening.

C. **Match the subjects with the predicates. Write the sentences on the lines below.**

Subject	Predicate
At the zoo, we	helps clean the cages.
The monkey	has a mane on its neck.
The African elephant	is black and white.
The zebra	likes to hang by its tail.
The male lion	visit the animals.
The tiger	is orange and black.
The zookeeper	is the largest living land animal.

1. _____

2. _____

3. _____

4. _____

5. _____

6. _____

7. _____

Context Clues

D. Read the story. Use the boldfaced words to fill in the blanks.

Cooking with Mom

Mom and I took out the **recipe** for Rice Krispie Cookies from the recipe **box**. The **ingredients** included Rice Krispies, marshmallows, and butter. We got the Rice Krispies and marshmallows from the **cupboard** and the butter from the **refrigerator**.

We heated the butter in a **pot** on the **stove**. When the butter was **melted**, we added the marshmallows. Then we stirred in the Rice Krispies. Lastly, we scooped the mixture out of the bowl and into a **square** pan.

1. A _____ gives directions for cooking.

2. My brother keeps his toys in a _____ .

3. The _____ are the things used in cooking something.

4. We often keep dry ingredients in a _____ .

5. I store butter in a _____ .

6. You can heat something in a _____ on a _____ until it is _____ .

7. Our cookie mixture went into a _____ pan.

Jane went out to play. She called on her friend, Sarah, but she wasn't at home. Then she went to Christine's house, but she wasn't at home either. Jane felt sad. There was no one to play with.

What Happens Next?

A. Write what you think will happen next. Give the story to a friend and ask him/her to write his/her ideas beside yours.

Your ideas	Your friend's ideas

Phonics: Vowel Digraphs – ai and ay

B. **Find the words with "ai" and "ay" that match the riddles.**

play	day	jay	paint	tray	tail

snail   say   pay   nail

1. I carry my house on my back.

_____

2. I have 24 hours.

_____

3. I hold things together when you are building.

_____

4. I am a blue bird.

_____

5. You can carry things on me.

_____

6. I make colourful pictures.

_____

7. I am found at the back of a dog.

_____

8. You must do this if you want to buy something.

_____

9. This is what you do when you speak.

_____

10. You like to do this with your friends.

_____

Word Order: Making Sentences

C. Rewrite the following groups of words to make sentences.

1. start autumn. We in school

    _____

2. home. close My is to school

    _____

3. to I from day. every walk and school

    _____

4. lunch. go I Sometimes, home for

    _____

5. sports at There school. of are lots my

    _____

6. volleyball. and soccer, play We hockey,

    _____

7. floor I games. to like play

    _____

Word Search

D. Find the words below in the word search.

snail may tray nail trail day
clay say hail play sail pray

q	w	f	s	w	h	o	f	x	f	h	k	t
h	b	k	n	e	b	k	r	b	h	l	g	r
r	o	x	a	l	m	n	o	k	l	w	z	a
p	k	f	i	q	a	g	z	l	z	s	n	i
q	g	c	l	a	y	o	c	z	n	a	i	l
r	o	e	q	c	d	k	d	r	f	y	j	h
b	h	q	t	e	l	f	e	s	w	e	h	f
q	x	o	r	v	b	p	r	a	y	r	l	n
z	d	r	a	f	w	f	w	d	n	p	q	l
p	l	a	y	w	o	x	o	r	s	t	i	s
s	t	x	x	h	e	d	x	h	x	a	x	h
g	d	h	b	o	l	k	b	c	h	r	i	m
r	a	o	f	r	b	s	l	e	t	s	g	l
h	y	m	l	x	m	l	b	x	n	a	y	b

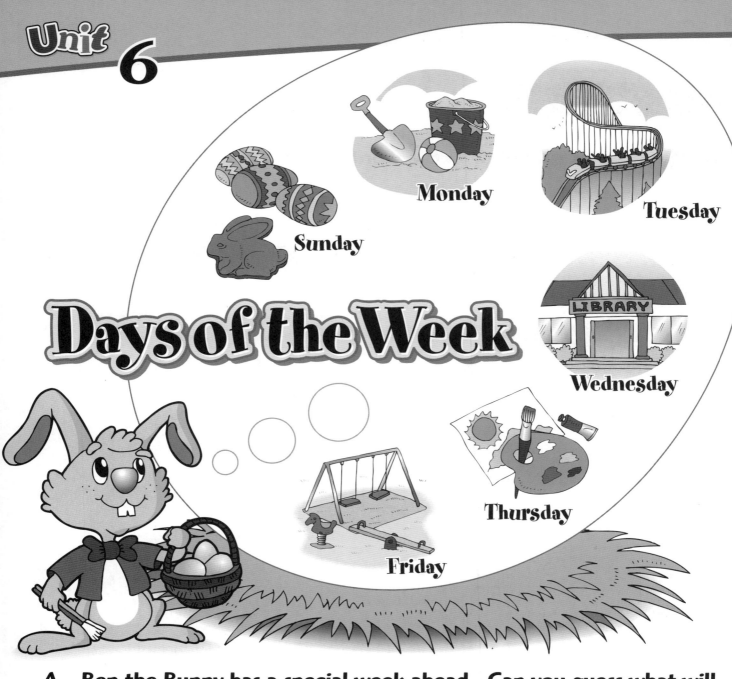

Unit 6

Days of the Week

A. Ben the Bunny has a special week ahead. Can you guess what will happen on each day? Finish the sentences.

1. On Sunday, it will be Easter.

2. On Monday, Ben _____

3. On Tuesday, _____

4. On Wednesday, _____

5. On Thursday, _____

6. On Friday, _____

7. Draw a picture of something you think Ben would like to do on Saturday and complete the sentence.

Saturday

On Saturday, _____

_____

_____

_____

_____

Phonics: Vowel Digraphs – ea and ee

B. Underline the correct word that fits each sentence.

1. The bee   beat makes its home in a hive.

2. The blue jeans   beans are hanging on the line.

3. It's nice to have a cup of tea   tee .

4. The baseball teem   team plays in summer.

5. The bean   been plant grew very high.

6. We will have some meat   meet for dinner.

7. Mom is going to weed   week the garden.

8. There are seven days in a weak   week .

9. We sail our boat on the sea   see .

10. This seed   seek will grow into a plant.

Unit 6

Telling (Declarative) Sentences

- A **Telling Sentence** tells you something.
- It begins with a capital letter and ends with a period (.).
  Example: Bees get nectar from flowers.

C. Colour the picture and write four sentences about what you see.

1. _____

   _____

   _____

2. _____

   _____

   _____

3. _____

   _____

   _____

4. _____

   _____

   _____

   _____

Unscrambling Words

D. **Unscramble the words and write them in the correct order on the lines.**

ptmeSereb · yaM · udseTay · raaJuny · yJlu

cmbeDeer · ydaFir · suAutg · eJnu · sneWdeyda

cObreto · nSdyua · yeFbuarr · odyaMn · crhaM

shTuyard · vmNeorbe · udraStya · lArpi

Months of the Year

_____

_____

_____

_____

_____

_____

_____

_____

Days of the Week

The days of the week and months of the year begin with a capital letter.

_____

_____

_____

_____

_____

The CN (Canadian National) Tower in Toronto, Canada is the tallest self-supporting tower in the world. It is as high as five and a half football fields and has a foundation that is as deep as a five-storey building.

The CN Tower was built to improve the broadcasting of radio and television signals. Many people have used it to break world records, like the person who hopped down its 1,967 steps on a pogo stick.

THE CN Tower

A. Read the story. Finish the sentences.

1. The CN Tower is the tallest _____

_____

2. It is as high as _____

3. Its foundation is _____

4. The CN Tower was built to _____

_____

5. One of the world records at the CN Tower was _____

_____

Phonics: Consonant Blends – bl, cl, fl, gl, pl, and sl

B. Write the missing consonant blends in the blanks.

| bl | cl | fl | gl | pl | sl |

1. Robert picked ____owers from the garden.

2. Michael saw the ____owns at the circus.

3. The children played on the ____ide.

4. His new car is ____ack.

5. The ____ass broke into many pieces.

6. They took the ____ed out in the winter.

7. There is a Canadian ____ag in front of our school.

8. Clare ____ew out the candles on the cake.

9. Maggie put the cookies on the ____ate.

10. They were ____ad they took their time.

11. The ____ock in the hall struck midnight.

12. At recess, we ____ay outside.

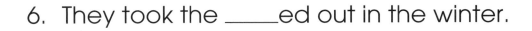

Asking (Interrogative) Sentences

- An **Asking Sentence** asks a question.
- It begins with a capital letter and ends with a question mark (?).
  Example: What does your spaceship look like?

C. Albert the Alien has just arrived on Earth. If you could ask him five questions, what would they be?

1. _____

   _____

   _____

2. _____

   _____

3. _____

   _____

4. _____

   _____

5. _____

   _____

Ask a friend to pretend that he or she is Albert and answer your questions.

Identifying Polygons

A polygon is a shape with 3 or more sides.

D. **In each case, draw the shape that matches the description.**

1. A polygon with 3 sides

2. A polygon with 4 sides

3. A polygon with 6 sides

4. A polygon with 7 sides

5. A polygon with 5 sides

6. A polygon with 8 sides

triangle

quadrilateral

pentagon

hexagon

heptagon

octagon

Sir John A. Macdonald

The first prime minister of Canada was Sir John A. Macdonald. He was born in Glasgow, Scotland in 1815 and came to Kingston, Ontario in 1820 at the age of five. He became a lawyer in 1836.

In 1867, the Dominion of Canada was formed with Sir John A. as its head. He was best known for his part in the completion of the Pacific Railway. He died in 1891 in Ottawa, the nation's capital.

A. Read the story and give short answers to the questions.

1. Who was the first prime minister of Canada?

   _____

2. Where was he born?

   _____

3. How old was he when he came to Ontario?

   _____

4. What year was the Dominion of Canada formed?

   _____

5. What was Sir John A. best known for?

   _____

Phonics: Consonant Blends – br, cr, dr, fr, gr, pr, and tr

B. Choose the consonant blends on the bricks below to fill in the blanks.

br   cr   dr   fr   gr   pr   tr

_____ une	_____ ime	_____ op
_____ ip	_____ ape	_____ ing
_____ eam	_____ uit	_____ aid
_____ ass	_____ one	_____ ize
_____ ap	_____ ee	_____ og
_____ um	_____ ess	_____ uck
_____ ab	_____ ail	_____ ue
_____ oom	_____ eed	_____ ame
_____ een	_____ ime	_____ oss
_____ ee	_____ ail	_____ oom

Surprising (Exclamatory) Sentences

- Wow! A **Surprising Sentence** is a sentence that shows strong feeling.
- It begins with a capital letter and ends with an exclamation mark (!).

C. Read the sentences below. What would you say in each case? Write the exclamations.

1. You found a $10 bill on the ground.

   _____

2. You learned to ride a two-wheeler.

   _____

3. You have just read your first book.

   _____

4. You just learned to swim.

   _____

5. You have a new puppy.

   _____

6. You won the first prize.

   _____

7. You are going to Disney World.

   _____

Ordinal Numbers

- **Ordinal Numbers** *are words that state the order of people or things.*

D. Look at the pictures and their ordinal numbers. Complete the sentences below.

first

second

third

fourth

fifth

sixth

seventh

eighth

ninth

tenth

1. The football is _____ .

2. The golf ball is _____ .

3. The baseball is _____ .

4. The volleyball is _____ .

5. The tennis ball is _____ .

6. The basketball is _____ .

7. The beach ball is _____ .

8. The shuttlecock is _____ .

9. The hockey puck is _____ .

10. The ping-pong ball is _____ .

Dance Lessons

dance   ten
jive   fun
good   day
many
slippers   ballet
costumes

A. Read the story. Choose the words that fit in the blanks.

When Kathleen was three years old, she started to learn 1._____ . She wore a pink leotard and tiny ballet 2._____ . She practised the steps every 3._____ .

By the time she was 4._____ years old, she was very good at ballet. She learned 5._____ new steps and routines. In no time at all, she was very 6._____ at jazz, too!

Later, when Kathleen was eighteen, she saw a 7._____ competition on television. She liked the dancers and the 8._____ , too. The people were the same age as she and they were having 9._____ . Now, Kathleen is learning the 10._____ .

Phonics: Consonant Blends – sk, sm, sn, sp, st, and sw

B.   Circle the correct consonant blends.

1.   Yum! That meat really st sm ells good!

2.   There are many galaxies in outer sk sp ace.

3.   There are two sets of sw st airs in our house.

4.   Mom cooked dinner on the st sn ove.

5.   Oh, no! There's a st sk unk by the tree.

6.   The sm sn ake slithered in the grass.

7.   What is your sm sn ack for recess?

8.   We will go for a sw sp im.

9.   She can sp sk ip with a rope.

10. The st sm all child was shy.

11. Kathleen tried to sk sw at the fly.

12. She tried to sp sn ip the thread with the scissors.

13. Can you sm sn ap your fingers?

14. I set the table with a fork, a knife, and a sm sp oon.

Imperative (Command) Sentences

• A **Command** is a sentence that tells someone to do something.

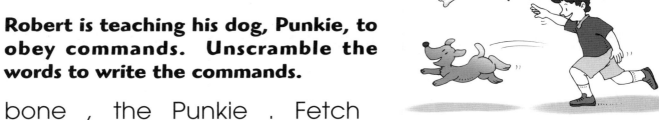

C. Robert is teaching his dog, Punkie, to obey commands. Unscramble the words to write the commands.

1. bone , the Punkie . Fetch

_____

_____

2. newspaper . and Punkie , get the go

_____

_____

3. shoe . Find Punkie , the

_____

_____

4. mouth . leash Take in the your

_____

_____

5. toy . the Find

_____

_____

6. chase Don't the car .

_____

_____

D. Help Sunny solve the riddles below.

Toonies, Loonies, and Such

| penny | nickel | dime | quarter | loonie | toonie |

1. I am worth 1¢.
   I am smaller than a nickel
   but bigger than a dime.
   I have maple leaves.

   _____

2. I am worth $2.00.
   I am silver and gold.
   I am the largest coin.

   _____

3. I am worth 10¢.
   I am the smallest coin.
   I have a schooner called
   the Bluenose.

   _____

4. I am worth 25¢.
   I am larger than a nickel but
   smaller than a loonie.
   I have a caribou.

   _____

5. I am worth $1.00.
   I am golden.
   I have a loon on the front.

   _____

6. I am worth 5¢.
   I am silver.
   I am larger than a dime but
   smaller than a quarter.

   _____

 **Word Families**

Change one letter.

A. Read the word at the beinning of each group. Read the sentences. Fill in rhyming words that make sense.

1. road   – They drove down the _____ .

    – The _____ and the frog are friends.

    – He lifted the _____ of bricks.

2. like   – I _____ to eat at McDonald's.

    – Mary rode her _____ to the store.

    – Dad and I went for a _____ .

    – _____ is a kind of fish.

3. game – We played a _____ of chess.

    – She _____ to my birthday party.

    – The baby lion is very _____ .

    – Her _____ is Judy.

4. bake – She will _____ some cookies for us.

    – Will you _____ your umbrella today?

    – The _____ is delicious.

    – The _____ is clear and blue.

    – Mom told David to _____ the lawn.

5. day – It is a beautiful _____ .

– _____ is a type of bird.

– The first _____ of sunshine beat down.

– Did she _____ where she was going?

– They found their _____ home.

– Her birthday is in the month of _____ .

Beginning, Middle, and Ending Consonants

B. Fill in the missing consonants.

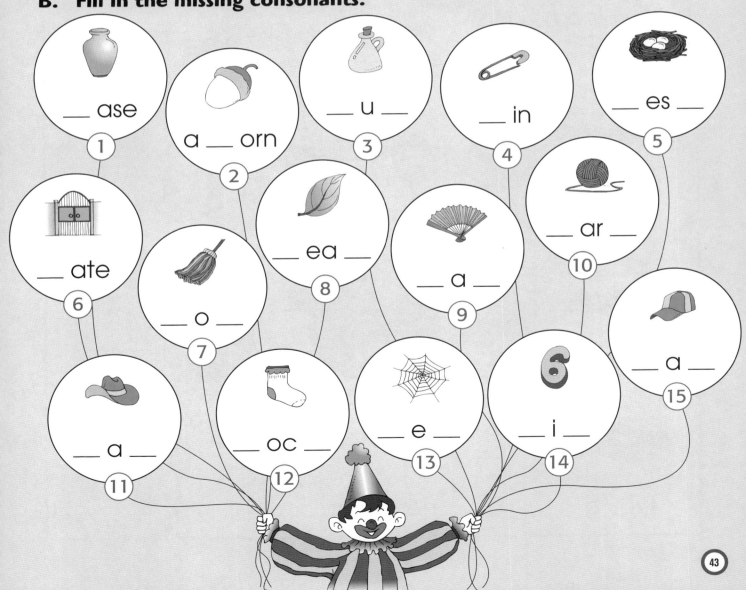

__ ase
1

a __ orn
2

__ u __
3

__ in
4

__ es __
5

__ ate
6

__ o __
7

__ ea __
8

__ a __
9

__ ar __
10

__ a __
11

__ oc __
12

__ e __
13

__ i __
14

__ a __
15

Short and Long Vowels

C. David loves baseball. Help him reach home base by filling in the missing vowels.

The Baseball Game

12. h __ nd

11. f __ ve

10. r __ ke

9. c __ be

3rd

1. t __ be

8. f __ sh

2. c __ ke

7. t __ nt

1st

2nd

3. l __ g

4. b __ ne

5. p __ le

6. h __ ve

44

Vowel Digraphs and Consonant Blends

D. Find the words listed below in the word search.

flag	tray	blue	reed	fruit	pail
slide	weed	cream	play	plate	snake
dream	tree	glass	clock	bean	stove
week	prize	grass	broom	tail	been

y	l	w	g	w	t	r	a	y	q	x	p	z	p	z	s
x	w	e	k	x	a	h	i	x	p	d	w	f	e	k	d
f	h	h	i	c	i	x	t	a	b	k	o	p	r	i	b
l	t	p	a	i	l	k	e	f	c	x	c	l	o	c	k
a	w	l	o	z	s	i	v	r	i	u	o	a	v	d	c
g	l	a	s	s	t	h	t	o	d	s	r	t	f	m	i
z	t	y	m	o	o	d	u	w	b	l	u	e	m	i	x
p	y	x	s	t	v	o	j	m	e	i	n	f	c	k	b
s	n	a	k	e	e	n	r	o	e	d	e	j	n	b	r
p	w	o	o	r	x	b	e	a	n	e	k	a	i	a	o
o	c	w	f	x	i	c	e	q	x	j	q	u	w	q	o
o	j	s	p	w	e	e	d	y	u	w	y	w	e	u	m
n	b	z	i	e	h	l	k	o	i	a	f	h	q	a	c
v	l	d	r	e	a	m	s	r	x	l	r	l	c	b	o
e	v	s	w	k	t	h	t	s	h	v	u	t	r	e	e
w	h	z	d	w	c	x	j	b	p	r	i	z	e	x	g
o	j	o	w	g	p	e	z	i	g	x	t	g	a	g	o
g	r	a	s	s	x	v	h	q	c	o	s	z	m	d	x

Sentences

E. **Give each sentence a correct punctuation and circle "T" for telling, "A" for asking, "S" for surprising, and "I" for imperative.**

1.	Kate loves chocolate cake	T	A	S	I
2.	Will David sweep the floor	T	A	S	I
3.	Open the door	T	A	S	I
4.	Do you like ice cream	T	A	S	I
5.	Oh, no	T	A	S	I
6.	Don't talk to strangers	T	A	S	I
7.	I won the first prize	T	A	S	I

Identifying Subjects and Predicates

F. **Circle the subjects and underline the predicates.**

1. The car drove down the highway.

2. The bird laid the eggs in the nest.

3. Mom bakes great cakes at home.

4. Tom walks to school every day.

5. She likes to take the dog for a walk.

The subject tells whom or what the sentence is about. The predicate tells what the subject is doing.

Subject / Predicate Match-up

G. Match the subjects with the predicates by writing the letters in the boxes.

1. The clown ☐   A. came down from the sky.

2. Dad ☐   B. wore face make-up.

3. A train ☐   C. chugged along the tracks.

4. Five frogs ☐   D. jumped on the lily pad.

5. My school ☐   E. has a big gymnasium.

6. Leaves ☐   F. often turn colours in autumn.

7. A comet ☐   G. gave me a big hug.

H. For each sentence, fill in the blanks to complete the subject and the predicate.

1. The _____ _____ to the beach.

2. An _____ _____ a fruit.

3. Many _____ _____ to the farm daily.

4. Every _____ , we _____ to the lunchroom.

5. Each _____ , they _____ skiing.

6. A _____ _____ a vehicle.

The Treasure Chest

Dear Dave,

We went to Sharaz last Thursday. When we arrived, we heard about a sunken ship in the shallow sea. The story goes like this – a pirate ship sank there long ago and there are still treasure chests aboard.

We decided to search for the sunken treasure. First, we boarded a small boat and rowed out to the ship. Then, we put on wetsuits and masks and dived under the water.

When we reached the ship, we swam inside and, guess what? We found a giant chest filled with gold and jewels!

I'll send you some photos as soon as I get them.

Your friend,
Rob

A. Read the letter and answer the questions.

1. What is the main idea of the first paragraph?

   _____

   _____

2. What is the main idea of the second paragraph?

   _____

   _____

Phonics: Consonant Digraphs – ch, sh, th, and wh

B. Fill in the missing letters to make tongue twisters.

> Tongue twisters with ch, sh, th, and wh are sometimes hard to say.

ch 1. _____ ester _____ ewed the _____ ewing gum _____ eerily.

sh 2. _____ e sells sea _____ ells by the sea _____ ore.

th 3. _____ addeus _____ ought _____ e _____ imble was _____ ick.

wh 4. Willy the _____ ale _____ irled _____ ile the _____ eel of the _____ ite _____ aler _____ istled.

C. In each case, choose the word that fits.

1. A cat's _____ help her find her way. (whisper, whiskers)

2. This gravy is _____ . (thick, think)

3. The _____ sank in the sea. (ship, shop)

4. The treasure _____ was filled with jewels. (cheat, chest)

5. The _____ is a delicious fruit. (beach, peach)

6. A _____ flies toward light. (moth, math)

Common Nouns

- A **Common Noun** names any person, place, or thing.
- It can be singular (one) or plural (more than one).

D. Add "s" to write the plural form of the singular nouns.

1. dog _____

2. mat _____

3. acorn _____

4. desk _____

5. ship _____

6. table _____

7. bear _____

8. girl _____

9. ruler _____

10. lake _____

11. boat _____

12. road _____

13. toy _____

14. tree _____

15. flower _____

16. plant _____

17. rug _____

18. flag _____

19. boy _____

20. mask _____

Baby Animals

E.   Read the sentences. Look at the pictures and fill in the blanks.

deer   dog   horse   goose   cat   pig
chicken   rabbit   cow   kangaroo

1.   A foal is a baby _____ .

2.   A calf is a baby _____ .

3.   A leveret is a baby _____ .

4.   A puppy is a baby _____ .

5.   A joey is a baby _____ .

6.   A piglet is a baby _____ .

7.   A chick is a baby _____ .

8.   A gosling is a baby _____ .

9.   A kitten is a baby _____ .

10.   A fawn is a baby _____ .

A Visit to the Farm

There are many different kinds of farms. Some are dairy farms and some are cattle farms. There are others that grow vegetables, like corn, potatoes, and carrots. In the West, farmers grow wheat.

Our class visited a farm. It was a dairy farm, so the animals were all cows. The farmer showed us how the cows are milked using big machines.

We had lots of fun at the farm.

A. Answer the questions.

1. What is the main idea of the first paragraph?

   _____

2. What kind of farm did the children visit?

   _____

3. What did the farmer use to milk the cows?

   _____

Phonics: R-controlled Vowels

- *When the letter "r" follows a vowel, it changes the sound of the vowel.*

B. Arnie the Farmer is going to the market. Help him get there. Underline the correct words.

Arnie's (form, farm) is (for, far) from the (market, marked). Every day, Arnie (works, worms) very (hard, harm). He (turms, turns) the soil, which is sometimes called (dirt, diet). When there are lots of (warms, worms) in the soil, it is healthy. There are also lots of animals on the (form, farm). Some are (horns, horses) and others are pigs, from which Arnie gets (park, pork) to sell at the market.

Proper Nouns

- A **Proper Noun** names a specific person, place, or thing.
- It always begins with a capital letter.

C. Colour the pages of the books that contain proper nouns.

1. boy / Mark

2. Ottawa / city

3. Venus / planet

4. Mrs. Smith / mother

5. Sun / star

6. dog / Punkie

7. Portland Drive / street

8. Mars / chocolate bar

9. Canada Day / holiday

10. day / Sunday

11. The Gap / store

12. Charlotte's Web / book

13. Deer Lake / town

14. month / May

Countries and Languages

D. Fill in the blanks.

Country	Language
Spain	Spanish
Italy	Italian
France	French
Greece	Greek
Canada	English
Romania	Romanian
Hungary	Hungarian

Many countries in the world have people who speak 1._____ , such as Canada. In Spain, people speak 2._____ and in 3._____ , people speak French. In the Eastern European countries of Hungary and Romania, people speak 4._____ and 5._____ . In Italy and Greece, people speak 6._____ and 7._____ .

E. Unscramble these languages.

LIAANTI	HASPNSI	GRHUAIANN
1	2	3
_____	_____	_____

Unit 12

Out on the Road

A. Time to Nibble
B. Home Sweet Home
C. Time for a Drink
D. Derek Turns the Curve
E. On the Straight and Narrow
F. Derek Hits the Fence

A. Derek the Dog is out on the road. Help him find his way home. Match the story titles below with the pictures in the maze. Print the letters in the boxes.

1

2

3

4

5

6

Phonics: Diphthongs – ou and ow

- **Diphthongs** are two vowel sounds that make a new sound.

B. **Say the words in the clouds below and print them where they belong.**

hound   grow   blow   row   blouse

couch   glow   town   brown   rainbow

mouse   low   flowers   crown   sound

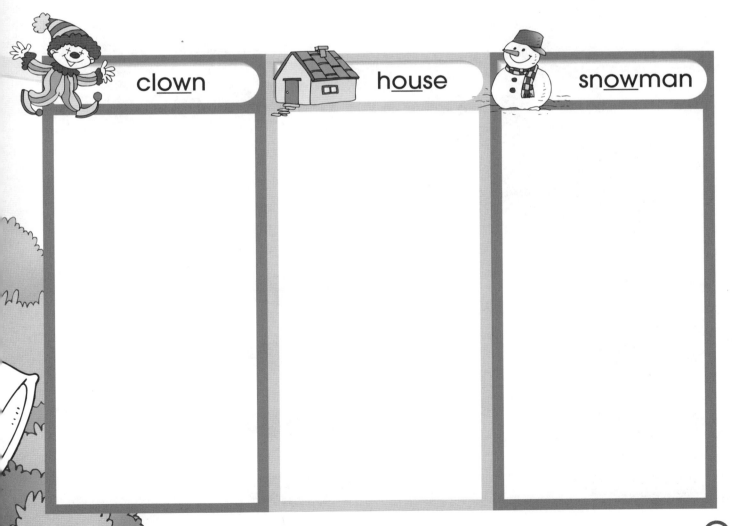

cl<u>ow</u>n   h<u>ou</u>se   sn<u>ow</u>man

 **Plural Nouns**

C. Look at the picture. Find the objects listed below. Count them and write the number words with the plural nouns.

street light

car

flower

boy

bicycle

tree

parking meter

truck

Homonyms

- **Homonyms** are word pairs that sound the same but have different meanings and are spelled differently.

D. Match the pictures and words with the homonyms.

1.  pear ☐

2.  sew ☐

3.  blue ☐

4. 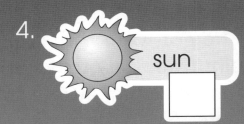 sun ☐

5.  see ☐

6. 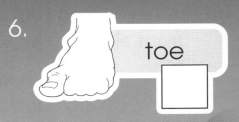 toe ☐

7.  flower ☐

8.  witch ☐

A. sea   B. blew   C. flour   D. tow

E. which   F. so   G. pair   H. son

The Coin Collection

David has a coin collection. He started it when he was six years old. He has over three hundred coins in his collection.

The first coins he got were three coins from Italy that his mom gave him after a trip there. Since then, many of his family members and friends have given him coins for gifts. He has coins from all over the world.

David's favourite coin is one from Sri Lanka. It is large and heavy. Another coin he likes is a Chinese one with a hole in the centre.

A. Read the story. Finish the sentences.

1. David has a _____

2. He has over _____

3. His first coins were _____

4. Many people have given _____

5. He has coins from _____

6. David's favourite _____

7. His favourite coin is _____

8. A Chinese coin has _____

Phonics: Diphthongs - oi and oy

- "**Oi**" and "**oy**" sound the same in words, but "oi" is usually found in the middle of a word and "oy" is usually found at the end.

B. **Read the sentences below. Fill in the blanks with words from the word bank.**

coin	toy	annoy	soy	oil
boy	joy	boil	point	loyal

1. Marie is a very _____ friend.

2. Christine has a _____ collection.

3. The _____ likes to play soccer.

4. Ryan gets a lot of _____ from playing sports.

5. The pencil has a very sharp _____ .

6. Some babies drink _____ milk.

7. Don't _____ your brother!

8. Will you _____ the water for tea?

9. The Game Boy is his favourite _____ .

10. _____ is lighter than water.

13

Verbs (Action Words)

- **Verbs** are words that describe actions.
  Example: running – She is running a race.

C. Find these actions in the picture and write a sentence using each one.

| swinging | playing | running | climbing | sliding |

1. _____

2. _____

3. _____

4. _____

5. _____

Synonyms

• **Synonyms** are words that mean the same thing.

D.   Read each sentence below. Circle the word that matches the one underlined.

1. Cindy was <u>weeping</u> when she fell down.

   crying   climbing

2. It was a <u>windy</u> day in the city.

   breezy   cool

3. Mom was <u>exhausted</u> after her trip.

   tired   trying

4. The <u>small</u> child held on to the balloon.

   little   large

5. The weather was <u>humid</u> and warm.

   damp   dry

6. The <u>huge</u> dog ran over to the car.

   big   tiny

7. The kiwi fruit were <u>firm</u> and green.

   hard   soft

8. The bike tires were <u>grimy</u> after they went through the mud.

   dirty   wet

1. Turn the oven up to 400° F.

2. Get these ingredients together.
   2 cups of flour
   1/2 cup of sugar
   1/2 cup of margarine (melted)
   1/2 tsp. of salt
   3 tsp. of baking powder
   1 cup of blueberries
   1 egg
   3/4 cup of milk

3. Put all the dry ingredients in a bowl.

4. Put all the wet ingredients in a bowl.

5. Mix the dry ingredients with the wet ingredients.

6. Spoon the mixture into a muffin pan.

7. Bake at 400° F for 15 – 20 minutes.

Making Blueberry Muffins

A. Read the cookbook recipe above. Circle the correct answers.

1. This recipe is for (muffins, cookies).

2. Milk is a (wet, dry) ingredient.

3. The fruit in this recipe is (blackberries, blueberries).

4. The seventh ingredient is (egg, milk).

5. The oven is turned up to (400°F, 400°C).

 Phonics: Special Sound "oo"

- *Words that have "**oo**" in them can sound like "oo" in "room" or "oo" in "cook".*

B.   Complete the rhymes with the words provided.

cookbook   cook   book   look

My mom taught me to 1._____

By reading a 2._____ .

She said, " Take a 3._____ .

This is called a 4._____ . "

fool   pool   drool   cool

The clown played the 5._____

Jumping in the 6._____ .

He thought it was 7._____

When he started to 8._____ .

"Being" Verbs (am, is, are)

- *"Am"*, *"is"*, and *"are"* are special verbs that tell about someone or something.

  Rules: Use *"am"* with *"I"*.

  Use *"is"* when it's one person, place, or thing.

  Use *"are"* when it's more than one person, place, or thing.

C.   Fill in the blanks with "am", "is", or "are".

1. Jason _____ riding his bike.

2. Kathleen and David _____ flying a kite.

3. She _____ planning to see the circus.

4. Maria _____ running to the bus.

5. There _____ three boys in the play.

6. They _____ best friends.

7. We _____ looking for the soccer ball.

8. I _____ going to the show with my dad.

9. Rob _____ driving his car.

10. It _____ a nice morning.

Antonyms

- **Antonyms** are words with opposite meanings.

D. Read the word inside each kite. Choose the correct antonym from the two words below it.

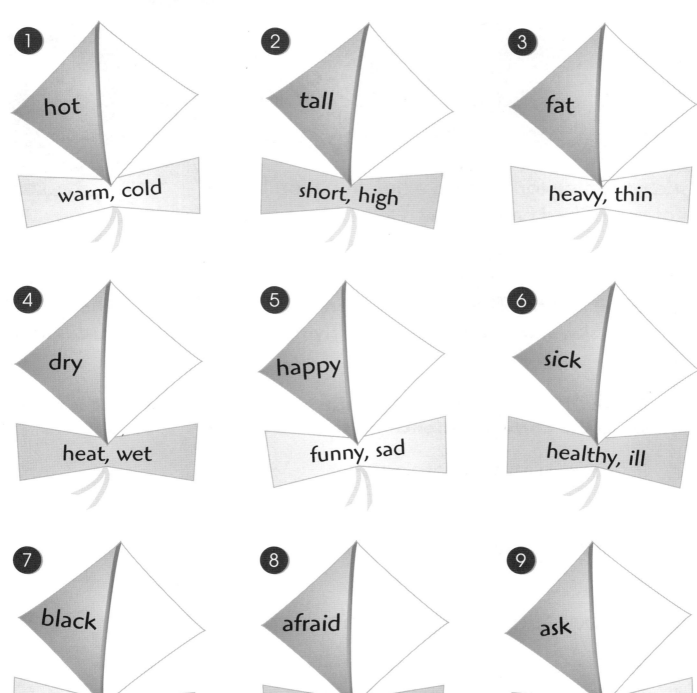

1 hot
warm, cold

2 tall
short, high

3 fat
heavy, thin

4 dry
heat, wet

5 happy
funny, sad

6 sick
healthy, ill

7 black
green, white

8 afraid
brave, scared

9 ask
question, answer

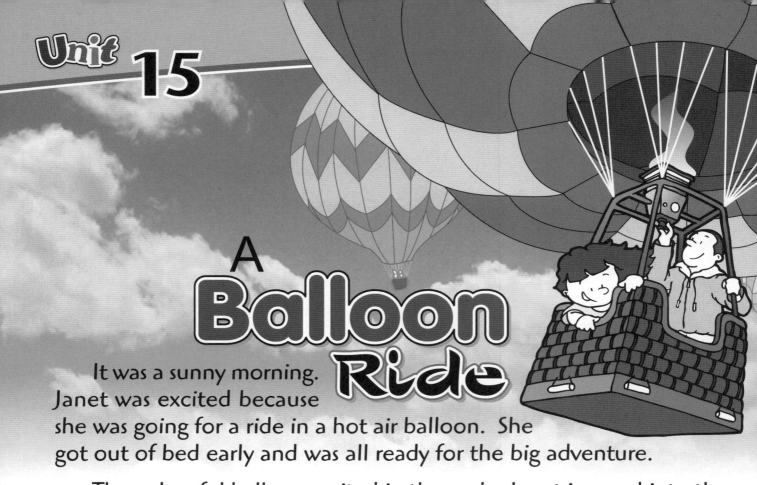

A Balloon Ride

It was a sunny morning. Janet was excited because she was going for a ride in a hot air balloon. She got out of bed early and was all ready for the big adventure.

The colourful balloon waited in the park. Janet jumped into the basket. She was ready to fly. The man in the basket used a burner to make the air hot. The balloon began to lift off slowly. Up they went into the sky. Janet felt like a bird flying over the tops of trees and houses.

A. Circle "T" for true or "F" for false to each sentence. If it is false, write the correct sentence on the line below.

1. It was a sunny afternoon.   T   F

   _____

2. The balloon was colourful.   T   F

   _____

3. The balloon was in the schoolyard.   T   F

   _____

4. The balloon lifted off quickly.   T   F

   _____

Phonics: Silent Consonants

- Some words have **Silent Consonants**. We don't hear the sound of the consonant when we say the word.

Example: Don't clim<u>b</u> up the tree.

B. Sometimes an "l" is silent. Add the silent "l" and say the words.

1. ha [ ] f

2. ta [ ] k

3. sta [ ] k

4. wa [ ] k

5. ca [ ] f

6. pa [ ] m

C. Answer the riddles with the silent "b" words.

lamb   limb   thumb   crumb

1. This is a young sheep. _____

2. You should keep this on your plate. _____

3. It is the finger that is nearest your wrist. _____

4. It is something found on some animals. _____

Subject-Verb Agreement

- The subject of a sentence must have a verb that "agrees".

D. **Read the facts about beavers. Choose the verb that agrees with the subject in each sentence.**

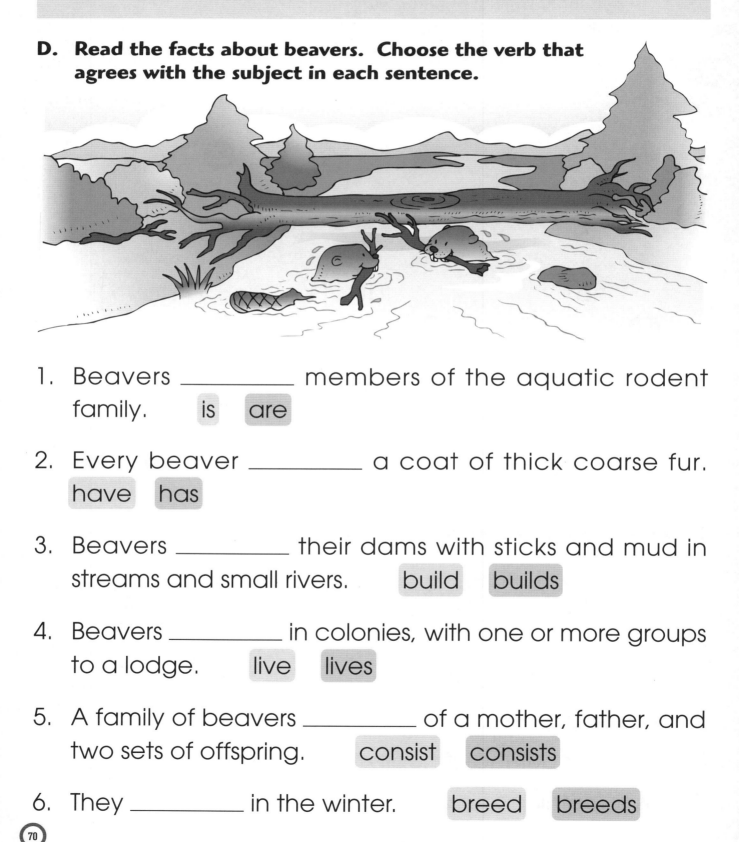

1. Beavers _____ members of the aquatic rodent family.   is   are

2. Every beaver _____ a coat of thick coarse fur.   have   has

3. Beavers _____ their dams with sticks and mud in streams and small rivers.   build   builds

4. Beavers _____ in colonies, with one or more groups to a lodge.   live   lives

5. A family of beavers _____ of a mother, father, and two sets of offspring.   consist   consists

6. They _____ in the winter.   breed   breeds

Antonyms

Antonyms are words with opposite meanings.

E. Find the antonyms in each sentence and write them on the lines below.

1. The hot air balloon needs cold air to land.

   _____   _____

2. Janet woke up early so that she would not be late for the balloon ride.

   _____   _____

3. The best time to fly a balloon is on a calm day and the worst time is on a windy day.

   _____   _____   _____   _____

4. Janet opened her eyes when the balloon went up but she closed them when it came down.

   _____   _____   _____   _____

It isn't really that easy.

F. Write a sentence using the antonyms "easy" and "hard".

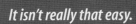

Autumn

carpet   beautiful   season
fall   fawns   summer
woods   because
colour   hike   animals
woods   ground

A.   Read the words above. Find the spaces where they belong in the story.

Autumn is the 1._____ that follows 2._____ .
Sometimes, we call it 3._____ . It is very 4._____
5._____ the leaves change 6._____ and fall to
the 7._____ . When they fall, the ground looks like a
8._____ .

It is fun to 9._____ in autumn. Often, there are lots
of 10._____ in the 11._____ in autumn. Baby deer
or 12._____ can be seen even in 13._____ near
cities.

B.   Answer the questions on the lines below.

1.   What season follows summer?

_____

2. What happens to leaves in autumn?

_____

3. Where do you find baby deer in autumn?

_____

4. What is another name for autumn?

_____

5. What season comes after autumn?

_____

Phonics: "Sad" Sounds – au and aw

• Both "**au**" and "**aw**" make the **Sad Sound**. When you say "saw" or "pause" out loud, you can hear why these are sad sounds.

C. Answer the questions with the correct words below.

jaw	autumn	yawn	auto
fawn	straw	saw	saucer

I saw a fawn open its jaws and yawn!

1. What is a baby deer? _____

2. What is part of your face? _____

3. What do you put in a drink? _____

4. What is another word for car? _____

5. What can be used to cut wood? _____

6. What season is also called "fall"? _____

7. What goes on the bottom of a cup? _____

8. What do you do when you are sleepy? _____

Adjectives

- An **Adjective** is a word that describes a person, place, or thing.
  Example: The <u>little</u> girl is wearing a <u>new</u> dress.

D. Underline the two adjectives in each sentence.

1. The tired boys rested under the shady tree.

2. He put a big book into a small bag.

3. The friendly nurse is helping the sick girl.

4. The old man is talking to the young child.

5. She picked a red apple from the tall tree.

6. The black puppy is playing with a red ball.

E. Use each pair of adjectives to make a sentence.

1. small and round
2. soft and fluffy
3. bright and colourful
4. long and thin

1. _____

2. _____

3. _____

4. _____

Homonyms, Synonyms, and Antonyms

F. Read the pair of words on each leaf. Decide if they are synonyms (S), homonyms (H), or antonyms (A). Circle the correct letter.

Homonyms are words that sound the same. Synonyms are words that have similar meanings. Antonyms are words with opposite meanings.

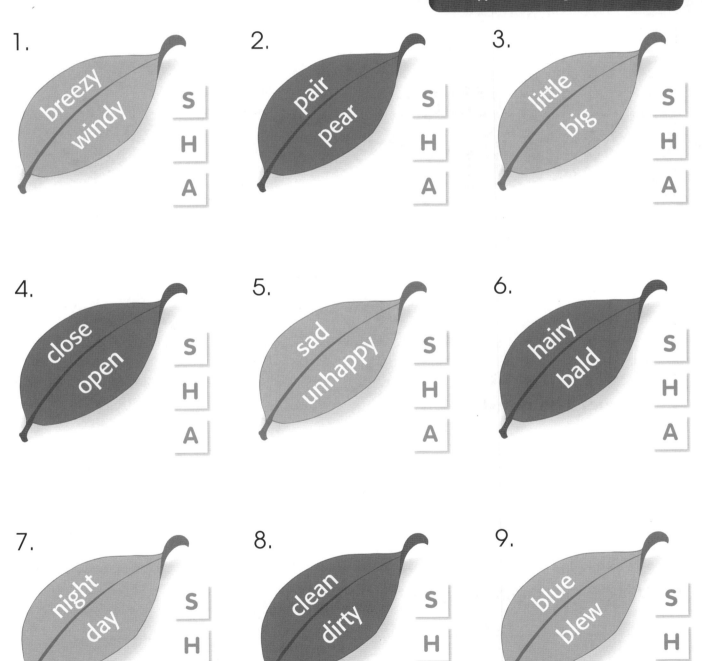

1. breezy / windy — S H A

2. pair / pear — S H A

3. little / big — S H A

4. close / open — S H A

5. sad / unhappy — S H A

6. hairy / bald — S H A

7. night / day — S H A

8. clean / dirty — S H A

9. blue / blew — S H A

Most plants start as a seed. Usually, you plant the seed in the garden or the yard, in shade or sun.

If you use a small trowel, you can dig a hole just big enough to poke the seed down and cover it with more soil.

First, you plant the seed and let the sun shine down on it. After a few weeks, little shoots begin to sprout. Then, the stem gets stronger and leaves begin to show.

All about Plants

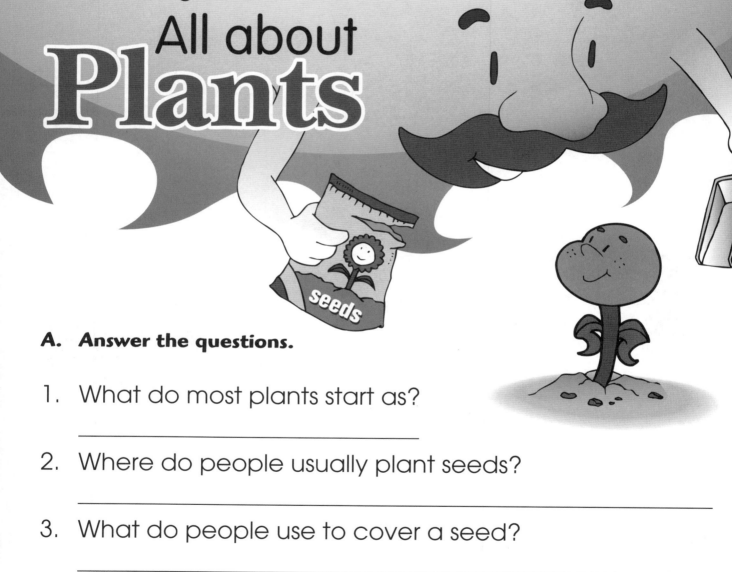

A.   Answer the questions.

1.   What do most plants start as?

   _____

2.   Where do people usually plant seeds?

   _____

3.   What do people use to cover a seed?

   _____

4.   How long does it take for shoots to sprout?

   _____

Phonics: Words with "y" as a Vowel

- Sometimes when "**y**" is at the end of a word, it sounds like an "e".
  Examples: many, only, penny

B. **Say the words on the left. Match them with the meanings.**

funny	another name for rabbit
buddy	causing laughter
carry	bright with sunshine
Mary	friend
bunny	a name for a girl
sunny	take something with you

C. **Fill in the missing words.**

 my   try   why   fly   shy

> Sometimes, the "y" at the end of a word sounds like an "i".

1. _____ did she go to the store?

2. Did you _____ to ride the bike?

3. We can _____ our kites another day.

4. The child was very _____ .

5. We can go to _____ house to play.

Past Tense Verbs

- Some verbs tell what happened in the past. You can add "**ed**" to them.

D. Add "ed" to the clue words and complete the crossword puzzle.

Across

A. plant
B. want
C. train
D. end
E. learn

Down

1. treat
2. sail
3. play
4. answer
5. need

Months of the Year

E.   Read the sentences below. Fill in the correct months.

October   July   January   June

November   April   December   February

March   May   August   September

1. In _____ , it is Christmas.

2. School starts in _____ .

3. Valentine's Day falls in _____ .

4. Halloween is at the end of _____ .

5. The first month of the year is _____ .

6. The month in which school ends for the summer vacation is _____ .

7. The eighth month of the year is _____ .

8. The second last month of the year is _____ .

9. St. Patrick's Day is in _____ .

10. This month rhymes with "day". _____

11. Canada Day is in this month. _____

Penguins

Penguins are birds that cannot fly but are good swimmers. They live in Antarctica and off the coasts of Africa and Australia. The smallest penguin is 40 cm tall. It is called the Blue Fairy. The tallest penguin is the Emperor. It can be 120 cm tall.

Penguins feed on fish, squid, and small shrimp. They are the prey of leopard seals and killer whales. The female penguin lays an egg or two and goes off in search of food. While she is gone, the male hatches the eggs on his feet under a layer of fur.

A.   Read the story. Write the correct answers in the blanks.

1.   Penguins live in _____ and off the coasts of _____ and _____ .

2.   The smallest penguin is called the _____ .

3.   It is _____ tall.

4.   The tallest penguin is called the _____ .

5.   Penguins feed on _____ , _____ , and _____ .

6.   The _____ lays eggs and the _____ hatches them.

Phonics: Soft and Hard "c" and "g"

- The letters "**c**" and "**g**" have both **Soft** and **Hard Sounds**.
  Examples: celery (soft "c" sound); can (hard "c" sound)
  ginger (soft "g" sound); go (hard "g" sound)

B.   Read the words and place them in the correct ice floes below.

Irregular Past Tense Verbs

- Some verbs don't end in "ed".
  Examples: sing ➡ sang; speak ➡ spoke

C.   Match up the present and past tenses.

1.	write •	• thought
2.	drink •	• wrote
3.	ring •	• drank
4.	think •	• left
5.	drive •	• drove
6.	leave •	• rang

D.   Write the present form of the past tense verbs in the cakes.

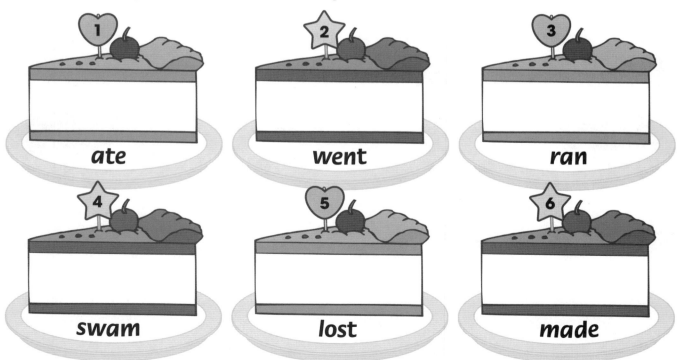

1. ate
2. went
3. ran
4. swam
5. lost
6. made

We use computers everywhere – at school, at home, at the doctor's, the dentist's, and the department stores. It is important to know the main parts of the <u>computer</u>. The <u>monitor</u> is the screen that displays words and pictures. When you type on a <u>keyboard</u>, your words appear on the monitor. If you want a paper copy, you can use a <u>printer</u> to print the words or pictures. Some computers use <u>diskettes</u> to save work and others use CDs, which look the same as the ones you use to play music. If you add a <u>modem</u> to your computer, you can communicate with other people.

Word Search

E. Circle the words that are underlined above.

z	b	y	d	i	s	k	e	t	t	e	s
o	u	n	o	q	c	k	b	s	j	x	c
j	p	r	i	n	t	e	r	a	l	b	o
k	d	b	i	a	b	y	o	f	e	u	m
o	e	a	u	e	u	b	h	c	j	i	p
r	u	f	c	r	m	o	d	e	m	b	u
i	c	t	d	s	c	a	o	n	e	r	t
m	o	n	i	t	o	r	d	k	e	l	e
j	v	s	i	w	o	d	h	g	s	k	r

A. Fill in the blanks with the words below.

smell   plates   small
oceans   weigh
length   chew   pitches
whole   breathing

Whales live in 1._____ throughout the world. Some whales have between 2 and 300 teeth, while others have no teeth at all. The whales that have no teeth feed on 2._____ organisms and use long bristles called 3._____ to eat them. Those that have teeth do not 4._____ their prey but eat them 5._____ .

Whales range in 6._____ from 1.3 metres to almost 30 metres. They 7._____ anywhere from 45 kg to 136,000 kg. Some whales have little sense of 8._____ and some none at all. Their hearing, however, allows them to hear 9._____ much higher than what we can hear.

Small whales can hold their breath for several minutes, and larger ones stay underwater without 10._____ for many hours.

A visit to the
Hockey Hall of Fame

A common noun names any person, place, or thing. A proper noun names a specific person, place, or thing.

B. Read the story. Circle the common nouns. Underline the proper nouns.

David and his friend, Judy, are going to visit the Hockey Hall of Fame in downtown Toronto, Canada. It is in a large building not far from Union Station, where the friends are taking the subway from Mississauga to Toronto.

There are so many exciting exhibits at the Hockey Hall of Fame. There are pieces of equipment worn by famous hockey players, like Wayne Gretzky. The Stanley Cup, which is awarded to the top hockey team each year, is sometimes on display there.

The children want to see the first mask that was worn by Jacques Plante and some of the old hockey uniforms from years gone by. Maybe, if they're lucky, they might see a visiting hockey player.

The last thing David and Judy go to see is all the statistics of players who broke many records over the years. Players like Gordie Howe, Jean Beliveau, and Wayne Gretzky changed the game of hockey forever.

Using Code

C. Use the code to fill in the blanks.

A	B	C	D	E	F	G	H	I	J	K	L	M	N	O
1	2	3	4	5	6	7	8	9	10	11	12	13	14	15

P	Q	R	S	T	U	V	W	X	Y	Z
16	17	18	19	20	21	22	23	24	25	26

___ ___ ___ ___ ___ ___ is one of the
 3   1   14   1   4   1

___ ___ ___ ___ ___ ___ ___ countries in the world. It is
12 1   18   7   5   19 20

one of three countries that make up

___ ___ ___ ___ ___   ___ ___ ___ ___ ___ ___ ___ . It is
14 15 18 20   8   1   13   5   18   9   3   1

made up of ___ ___ ___ provinces and
            20   5   14

___ ___ ___ ___ ___ territories. ___ ___ ___ ___ ___ ___ ___
20   8   18   5   5   14   21   14   1   22   21   20

became the newest territory in 1999.

There are ___ ___ ___ ___ Atlantic provinces and
           6   15   21   18

___ ___ ___ ___ ___ of them are called
20   8   18   5   5

___ ___ ___ ___ ___ ___ ___ ___ provinces.
13   1   18   9   20   9   13   5

There are also ___ ___ ___ ___ ___ Prairie provinces.
                20   8   18   5   5

 **Grammar Focus**

D. Circle the correct answers.

1. Maria is / are from the Philippines.

2. Frank and I like / likes to watch football.

3. David play / plays his guitar every day.

4. Kathleen studied / studyed hard before her exams.

5. May take / takes the dog for a walk daily.

6. They have / has lunch together.

7. That clown laugh / laughs loudly.

8. John is / am good at cooking.

9. Rob fix / fixed his own car.

10. I is / am hungry.

E. Make a sentence with each adjective.

1. tall

_____

2. beautiful

_____

3. friendly

_____

Vocabulary Building

Homonyms are words that sound the same but have different meanings.

F. Underline the correct homonyms.

1. sail (sale, seal)

2. see (sea, say)

3. pair (pear, peal)

4. male (mail, mane)

5. blew (blue, blow)

6. vain (vane, van)

G. Circle the synonym for each word below.

1. big (small / large)

2. weep (sweep / cry)

3. small (tiny / big)

4. dash (run / walk)

5. jump (hop / jog)

6. unhappy (sad / cheery)

Synonyms are words that have similar meanings.

H. Circle the correct antonyms.

1. dark (night / bright)

2. wet (dry / wide)

3. dirty (clean / muddy)

4. open (close / wide)

Antonyms are words that have opposite meanings.

5. sad (happy / mad)

6. light (heavy / easy)

Vowels that Sound like "e" or "i"

I. Colour "e" or "i" to show what the "y" in each word sounds like.

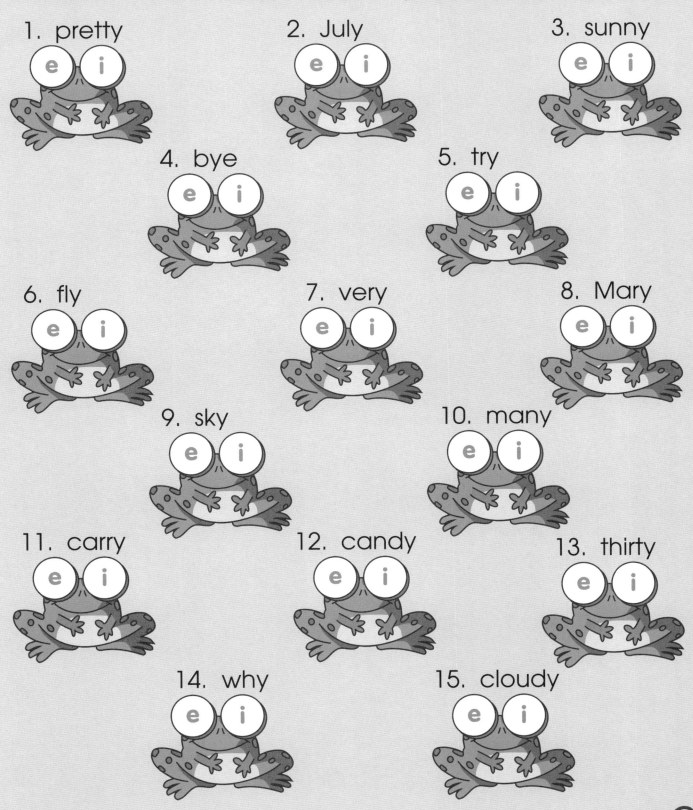

1. pretty   e i

2. July   e i

3. sunny   e i

4. bye   e i

5. try   e i

6. fly   e i

7. very   e i

8. Mary   e i

9. sky   e i

10. many   e i

11. carry   e i

12. candy   e i

13. thirty   e i

14. why   e i

15. cloudy   e i

Outside

Inside

Common and Proper Nouns

A **common noun** names any person, animal, place, or thing.

Examples: boy (a person)   dog (an animal)
                    city (a place)   game (a thing)

A **proper noun** names a specific person, animal, place, or thing. It always begins with a capital letter. Names that are given to people and pets are proper nouns.

Examples: Steven (a person)   Pug (an animal)
                    Edmonton (a city)   Monopoly (a thing)

A.   Write the nouns in the correct columns. Begin the proper nouns with capital letters.

Days of the week, months of the year, and festivals are also proper nouns.

| beatrice | lollipop | april | car |
| lake | christmas | thursday | rainbow |

Common Noun	**Proper Noun**
_____	_____
_____	_____
_____	_____
_____	_____

Singular and Plural Nouns

A **singular noun** names one person, animal, place, or thing.

Example: The <u>girl</u> likes playing with the <u>dog</u>.

A **plural noun** names more than one person, animal, place, or thing. Many plural nouns are formed by adding "s" to the singular nouns.

Example: The <u>girls</u> like playing with the <u>dogs</u>.

B. Write the noun under each picture. Change the singular noun to plural if the picture shows more than one.

kid

apple

parrot

sweet

chick

rat

1.

_____

2.

_____

3.

_____

4.

_____

5.

_____

6.

_____

Forming Plural Nouns

For nouns ending in "s", "x", "ch", or "sh", add "es" to form the plural.

Examples: bus → buses   beach → beaches

For nouns ending in "y", change the "y" to "i" and add "es".

Examples: lily → lilies   baby → babies

C. Complete the crossword puzzle with the plural form of the clue words.

Across

A. bench
B. box
C. glass
D. dress
E. wish

Down

1. fairy
2. brush
3. daisy

Countable and Uncountable Nouns

Some nouns are **countable**. You can use number words before their plural form.

Example: There are <u>five apples</u> in the basket.

Some nouns are **uncountable**. You cannot use number words before them and they do not have any plural form.

Example: <u>Milk</u> is good for us.

D. Circle the correct words for the sentences.

1. Audrey loves her new pet kitten / kittens .

2. Pour some water / waters into the two cup / cups .

3. Can you see those squirrel / squirrels in the tree?

4. The bottles are made of plastic / plastics .

5. Add some sand / sands to these pot / pots .

6. Grandpa gives me two dollar / dollars every day.

7. The little boy is sleeping on some fresh hay / hays in the barn / barns .

8. Mom wants to buy some new furniture / furnitures for our house.

unit 2 Pronouns

Subject Pronouns

A **pronoun** replaces a noun. A **subject pronoun** acts as the subject in a sentence.

"I", "you", "we", "he", "she", "it", and "they" are subject pronouns.

Example: Joshua is my classmate.
He is my neighbour too.

A. Circle the subject pronouns in these sentences.

1. We went to the movie last night.

2. Larry and I both like skiing.

3. I will give you a call.

4. He won't let us down.

5. We are visiting Calgary this summer. It is in Alberta.

6. I didn't know where the restaurant was. They showed me the way.

7. Melissa likes collecting coins. She keeps them in a big jar.

B. Write the subject pronouns for the words.

1. Ray and I _____

2. Mr. Hopkins _____

3. The squirrel _____

4. The flowers _____

5. Cindy _____

6. The sea _____

C. Replace the underlined words with subject pronouns.

1. <u>Mom and Dad</u> take us to the zoo.

   _____

2. <u>My family and I</u> go to see the zebras first.

   _____

3. <u>My brother Cecil</u> takes pictures of the zebras.

   _____

4. <u>One of the zebras</u> looks at us.

   _____

Object Pronouns

An **object pronoun** receives the action of the verb in a sentence.

"Me", "you", "us", "him", "her", "it", and "them" are object pronouns.

Example: Mrs. Lynch drives Keith to school.
Mrs. Lynch drives <u>him</u> to school.

D. Draw lines to join the nouns to the correct object pronouns.

us •

him •

her •

it •

them•

- my sister
- the cows
- the policeman
- Lily and me
- Kate's hamster
- Mr. and Mrs. Hall
- our class
- his tall hat
- the little girl
- Kevin the Clown

E. Choose the correct pronouns to complete the sentences.

1. Ginny has a dog. She walks (them / it) _____ in the park every day.

2. Do you want (I / me) _____ to get (you / me) _____ something to drink?

3. Hilda and Aaron are my best friends. I'll surely invite (her / them) _____ to my party.

4. Dennis is very upset. Do you know what happened to (him / us) _____ ?

5. Mr. Davidson promised to tell (us / we) _____ the ending of the story tomorrow.

6. Christine is sick. Mom is giving (her / she) _____ some medicine.

F. Look at the picture. Write sentences about it with the object pronouns.

us _____

_____

them _____

_____

it _____

_____

Articles

"A", "an", and "the" are **articles**. They come before nouns.
"A" is used before a noun that begins with a consonant sound.
"An" is used before a noun that begins with a vowel sound.
"The" is used before a noun that names a particular person, place, or thing. It is also used with something unique.

Examples: <u>a</u> girl   <u>an</u> honour   <u>the</u> GO Train   <u>the</u> moon

A. Put the words in the correct boxes.

South Pole   unit   RCMP   album   error
river   idea   umbrella   house
CN Tower   violin   St. Lawrence River

a	an	the

B. Draw lines to match the articles with the pictures. Then, write what each picture shows with the correct article. Use the words in the box.

unicorn   Earth   owl   rainbow
Olympic Games   airplane

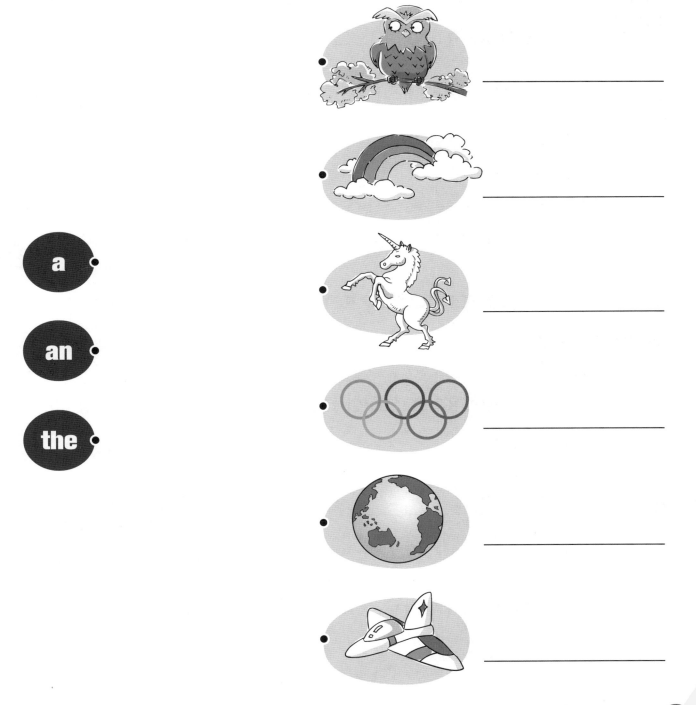

C. Fill in the blanks with the correct articles.

1. Do you know _____ girl over there?

2. Is this _____ orange or _____ grapefruit?

3. There are no penguins in _____ North Pole. You can only find them in _____ South Pole.

4. _____ Rockies lie between British Columbia and Alberta.

5. Look at _____ ape in _____ cage. Is it _____ chimpanzee?

6. We've forgotten to buy one of _____ ingredients. We need _____ avocado.

7. _____ friend should be one that cares about your feelings.

8. The train left _____ hour ago.

9. I wish I could fly in _____ sky.

An article can be used before a noun with an adjective.
Use "a" if the adjective begins with a consonant sound.
Use "an" if it begins with a vowel sound.
Use "the" if the noun with the adjective refers to a particular person, place, or thing.

Examples: <u>a</u> beautiful flower
<u>an</u> honest girl
<u>the</u> national anthem

D. Write an adjective on the line to describe the noun. Then write the correct article in the box.

icy
oval
huge
Great
Prime
unkind
European
Canadian

1. ☐ _____ elephant

2. ☐ _____ country

3. ☐ _____ table

4. ☐ _____ person

5. ☐ _____ flag

6. ☐ _____ road

7. ☐ _____ Minister

8. ☐ _____ Lakes

Present Tense Verbs

A **present tense verb** tells what happens now. Add "s" to the base form of the verb to tell about one person or thing.

Examples: My family and I <u>live</u> in Toronto.
My aunt <u>lives</u> in Hamilton.

Use the "ing" form of the verb with "am/is/are" to tell what someone or something is doing.

Example: The children are <u>reading</u>.

A. Complete the chart below.

Base Form	"s" Form	"ing" Form
1. sing		
2. start		
3.		listening
4. gather		
5.		walking
6.	laughs	
7. break		
8.	visits	

B. Circle the correct words for the sentences.

1. The sun shine / shines brightly.

2. The children are walk / walking along the pond.

3. They chat / chats happily.

4. Some ducks live / lives in the pond.

5. Derek is looks / looking at the ducks.

C. Check ✔ if the underlined words are correct. Write the correct words on the lines if they are wrong.

1. I <u>eats</u> toast for breakfast every day. _____

2. It <u>get</u> darker and darker. _____

3. We <u>stays</u> in the tent at night. _____

4. The wind is <u>blow</u> fiercely. _____

5. The bees are <u>collecting</u> nectar. _____

> ### Am, Is, and Are
>
> "Am", "is", and "are" are the present forms of the verb "be".
> Use "**am**" with "I".
> Use "**is**" to tell about one person, animal, place, or thing.
> Use "**are**" to tell about more than one person, animal, place, or thing.
>
> *Examples*:   I <u>am</u> a student.
>   A panda <u>is</u> black and white.
>   Mom's cookies <u>are</u> great.

D. Fill in the blanks with "am", "is", or "are".

1. Bees _____ busy insects.

2. Christmas _____ in December.

3. I _____ happy to see you again.

4. Popcorn _____ my favourite treat.

5. I _____ seven years old.

6. The ducks _____ very cute.

7. Where _____ my shoes?

"Am", "is", or "are" can be used with the "ing" form of verbs to tell what someone or something is doing.

Examples: I <u>am</u> watching TV.
He <u>is</u> having a good time.
They <u>are</u> making a kite.

E. Look at each picture and write a sentence about what is happening.

1.

_____

_____

2.

_____

_____

3.

_____

_____

4.

_____

_____

Past Tense Verbs

A **past tense verb** tells about something that happened in the past. For most verbs, add "d" or "ed" to the base form to change them to the past form.

Example: Thomas <u>folded</u> a paper crane this morning. He <u>used</u> blue paper to fold it.

A. Add "d" or "ed" to write the past form of the given verbs.

1 close

2 score

3 lift

4 brush

5 erase

6 reach

7 collect

8 dislike

Some past tense verbs are formed by repeating the last letter before adding "ed".

Example: Steven <u>slipped</u> on his way to school.

For verbs ending in "y", change the "y" to "i" before adding "ed".

Example: I <u>studied</u> until eleven last night.

B. Fill in the blanks with the correct form of the verbs to see what Dodo the Dog did yesterday.

hurry	grab	carry	stop
prefer	learn	try	skip

Dodo 1._____ a backpack

to school yesterday. He 2._____ some funny

tricks at the dog school. Then he 3._____ for an

hour. He 4._____ home for lunch after school.

On his way home, he 5._____ by a grocery

store and 6._____ some dog food. He also

7._____ to look for a bone as a treat, but

couldn't find one that he 8._____ .

Irregular Past Tense Verbs

Some past tense verbs do not end in "ed". They may spell the same as the base form or they may be completely different.

Example: He goes fishing every summer.
He <u>went</u> fishing last Sunday.

C. Complete the crossword puzzle with the past tense of the clue words.

Across

A. stand
B. teach
C. throw
D. weep

Down

1. catch
2. buy
3. burst
4. leave
5. speak
6. spread

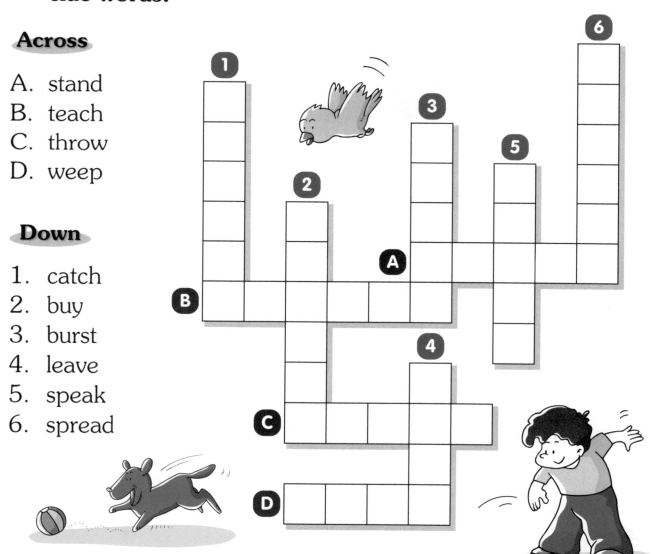

Was and Were

"**Was**" and "**were**" are the past forms of the verb "be".
Use "was" to tell about one person, animal, place, or thing.
Use "were" to tell about more than one person, animal, place, or thing.

Example: There <u>was</u> a rainstorm last night.

"Was" and "were" can also be used with the "ing" form of verbs to tell what someone or something was doing at a past time.

Example: We <u>were</u> having dinner when Uncle Sam visited.

D. Check ✔ if the underlined words are correct. Cross ✗ if they are wrong. Then correct the wrong sentences.

1. It <u>were</u> raining when he walked his dog. ◯

_____

_____

2. There <u>was</u> a bird in the tree this morning. ◯

_____

3. The kids <u>was</u> singing when the teacher came in. ◯

_____

4. Hilary and I <u>was</u> at the show last night. ◯

_____

Adjectives

An **adjective** tells about a noun. It often tells how a person, an animal, a place, or a thing looks. Colour words, number words, and shapes are all adjectives.

Examples: The <u>little</u> girl is <u>skinny</u>.
Bananas are <u>yellow</u>.
There are <u>three</u> pigs in the house.
I like that <u>square</u> clock.

A. Look at the pictures. Write what they are with the given words.

three
scary
tall
freezing
naughty
angry

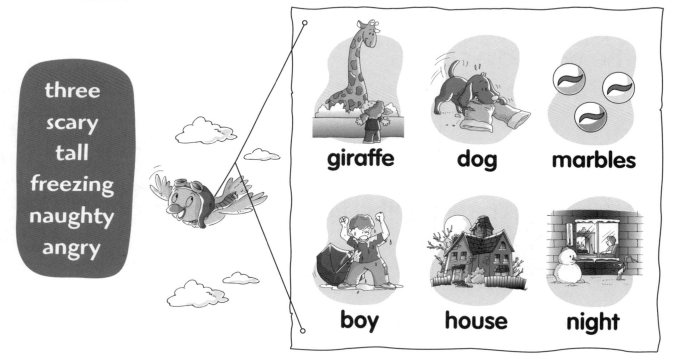

giraffe   dog   marbles

boy   house   night

1. a _____ giraffe   2. _____

3. _____   4. _____

5. _____   6. _____

B. Fill in the blanks with the given adjectives.

round　new　fresh　black
lazy　green　seven　juicy
puzzled　hot　white　yellow

1. It's such a _____ pig. It's always sleeping.

2. _____ apples are usually sour.

3. I want a _____ peach.

4. A rainbow has _____ colours.

5. Mom wants to buy a _____ table.

6. My brother likes eating _____ curry.

7. Do you see my _____ yoyo? I just bought it yesterday. It is _____ with a star in the middle.

8. Pandas are _____ and _____ bears. They only eat _____ bamboo shoots.

9. Sam looks _____ . He does not understand what his sisters are doing.

C. **Circle the adjectives in the sentences. Then think of other adjectives that can be used in the sentences. Write them in the boxes.**

You can change the meanings of the original sentences.

1. She looks pretty in that costume.

2. This is a very interesting story.

3. The dog has just given birth to six puppies.

4. The red roses in the yard were a gift from our neighbour.

5. The room was so hot that we couldn't stay there any longer.

6. I dreamed of a scary monster last night.

7. They strolled down the road in the scorching sun.

8. We went to the restaurant around the corner. The food there was great.

D. Colour the picture. Write six sentences with adjectives to describe it. Try to include colour words, number words, and shapes in your sentences.

1. _____

2. _____

3. _____

4. _____

5. _____

6. _____

A. Read the story. Circle ◯ the proper nouns.

Long, long ago, there was a <u>kingdom</u> called Colourland. The king, King Edwin, and his people did everything they could to make their kingdom a happy and colourful <u>place</u> to live in. Their only problem was a naughty little <u>elf</u> named Coby. Coby enjoyed playing <u>tricks</u> on the people of Colourland.

One day, Coby caused a lot of mischief – the people woke up to find that all <u>colours</u> were gone. Everything was now in black and white! They had lost the most precious thing they prided themselves on.

King Edwin and his people tried in vain to look for Coby, but they found a note on <u>parchment</u> left by him.

To get back all colours, Princess Lilian and Prince Ned have to search for things in different colours. When they have found each thing, one of them needs to touch or hold it in the <u>hands</u> and say its colour, and the other one has to say "Retrieve colour!" Then that colour will return to the kingdom. Remember, the thing must be whole and complete, and there is only one <u>chance</u> for each colour. If they say the wrong colour, that colour will be lost forever.

Good <u>luck</u>!

Coby

B. Read the story in (A) again. Put the underlined words in the correct places. Then complete what Coby says.

Countable

Singular:

Plural:

Uncountable

All these words are
_____ nouns.
common / proper

C. Fill in the blanks with the correct pronouns.

When Princess Lilian finished reading the note,

1. _____ said, "That's easy. 2. _____ saw a red

rose in the garden yesterday. Let's go, Ned. 3. _____

can retrieve the colour together right away." But before

4. _____ reached the palace door, King Edwin

shouted, "Look! Words are appearing on the

parchment." Ned ran back and took a look at the

line. 5. _____ read, "6. _____ can only find the

things in nature beyond Colourland." 7. _____ was

dumbstruck.

D. Circle the correct articles to complete the paragraphs below.

Lilian and Ned had never been to anywhere outside *1.* a / an / the kingdom before, so King Edwin said, "Wilkin, I'd like you to go with Lilian and Ned. I'm sure you'll be able to help them solve the problem." Wilkin was *2.* a / an / the son of the king's adviser. He was *3.* a / an / the very smart child. He had grown up with *4.* a / an / the prince and the princess, and they were good friends.

So *5.* a / an / the three children started their journey in search of *6.* a / an / the lost colours. Before they left the kingdom, they hoped that *7.* a / an / the world outside would still have colours, but they were disappointed. Not *8.* a / an / the tint of any colour was in sight.

9. A / An / The idea suddenly came to Ned's mind. "Let's look for *10.* a / an / the rainbow first. This can surely save us *11.* a / an / the trouble of searching for seven different things, right?"

Do you think this is *12.* a / an / the good idea?

E. Fill in the blanks with the correct present forms.

1. Ned _____ to look for a rainbow first.
   <u>want / wants</u>

2. Wilkin _____ they will not be able to find one.
   <u>says / saying</u>

3. Lilian and Ned _____ Wilkin for the reason.
   <u>ask / asks</u>

4. Wilkin _____ to them that they will not see a
   <u>explain / explains</u>

   rainbow when there _____ no colour.
   <u>is / are</u>

5. It _____ also impossible for them to touch or
   <u>is / are</u>

   hold a rainbow in their hands even if they

   _____ one.
   <u>find / finds</u>

6. The children _____ thinking of what they can
   <u>is / are</u>

   do.

7. Ned is _____ to and fro, and
   <u>paces / pacing</u>

   Lilian is _____ her nails.
   <u>bites / biting</u>

8. "Don't worry! I _____
   <u>is / am</u>

   sure we can solve the

   problem," Wilkin says with

   confidence.

F. Rewrite the sentences by changing the verbs in parentheses ( ) to the correct past forms.

1. The children (find) it hard to decide on what to look for first.

   _____

   _____

2. They (be) afraid that they (may) make the wrong guess.

   _____

   _____

3. They (stay) right beyond the kingdom for the whole afternoon.

   _____

   _____

4. The colourless sun (be + set) and it (be + get) dark.

   _____

   _____

5. The first day of their quest (slip) away quietly.

   _____

G. Fill in the blanks with the correct adjectives.

loud round blue small three happy
boring very colourless sweet sure

The 1._____ children woke up the next day and saw something 2._____ in the sky. It was the sun, but the sun could not make them 3._____ today.

Suddenly, a bird came flying into sight. Wilkin let out a 4._____ cry. "It's a 5._____ jay!"

"Are you 6._____ ?" Lilian asked hesitantly.

"Of course! I can recognize them even if they're 7._____ ," Wilkin said. Then he took out some bread and tore a 8._____ piece from it. He placed the piece in Lilian's hand, and started whistling a 9._____ tune.

The bird flew into Lilian's hand and ate the bread. The 10._____ moment it finished eating the bread, Lilian said, "Blue!" and Ned's "Retrieve colour!" followed. All of a sudden, the bird in Lilian's hand turned blue. They looked around them and saw patches of blue among the 11._____ black and white. They did it!

unit 7 Prepositions

Prepositions

Some **prepositions** are location words. They tell where people, animals, or things are.

Examples: Pete is <u>in</u> his own pet shop.
He wants to put the paper <u>on</u> the board.
The fish are <u>in</u> the tank.

A. Circle the prepositions in these sentences.

1. There are lots of stars in the night sky.

2. The shy little girl hides behind her mom.

3. Did you see that dog jump over the fence?

4. Hurry! He's waiting at the bus stop near the community centre.

5. Please leave the book on the desk by the window.

6. There is a bakery between the grocery store and the Italian restaurant.

7. There are some wildflowers under the bench beside the fountain.

B. Look at the picture. Fill in the blanks with the correct prepositions.

in   on   behind   beside   around   from

Samuel is 1.＿＿＿＿＿＿ an ocean liner. He is sitting 2.＿＿＿＿＿＿ a table 3.＿＿＿＿＿＿ the deck enjoying the cool breeze. There are some clouds 4.＿＿＿＿＿＿ the sky but the weather is still fine. There is a drink 5.＿＿＿＿＿＿ the table. Samuel does not know what is 6.＿＿＿＿＿＿ the glass but he thinks it tastes great. A little bird is 7.＿＿＿＿＿＿ Samuel. It seems to want to share this tranquil moment with him.

The ocean liner is not too far 8.＿＿＿＿＿＿ the shore. Samuel can see people tiny as ants 9.＿＿＿＿＿＿ the beach. There are some colourful sailboats drifting 10.＿＿＿＿＿＿ too.

Some prepositions tell when someone does something or when something happens.

Examples: We like going to the beach <u>in</u> summer.
We usually go there <u>on</u> weekends.
The sun is high up in the sky <u>at</u> noon.

C. Fill in the blanks with the correct prepositions.

1. Let's go to the movies _____ Friday night.
   _{in / on}

2. The flowers bloom _____ spring.
   _{in / at}

3. The baseball game starts _____ eight o'clock tonight.
   _{on / at}

4. We are planning on a trip to Cuba _____ November.
   _{in / on}

5. What are you going to dress up as _____ Halloween?
   _{in / on}

6. Why don't we talk about this _____ lunchtime?
   _{in / at}

7. Dad and his friends meet _____ the first day of every month.
   _{on / at}

D. Check ✔ if the underlined prepositions are correct. Correct the wrong ones on the lines.

1. Mom works out <u>in</u> Monday morning. _____

2. Uncle Ben will come to visit us <u>in</u> August. _____

3. The next train leaves <u>on</u> half past ten. _____

4. Macy was born <u>in</u> 1999. _____

5. The last gleam of sunlight fades <u>in</u> dusk. _____

6. We can go tobogganing <u>in</u> winter. _____

7. We have a big party <u>at</u> New Year's Eve. _____

8. They have to finish their project <u>on</u> a week. _____

9. The clock struck twelve <u>on</u> midnight. _____

10. Christmas is <u>in</u> December 25th. _____

11. They like decorating their home with colourful lights and a Christmas tree <u>at</u> Christmas.

    _____

12. They will unwrap their Christmas presents <u>at</u> Boxing Day.

    _____

unit 8 Sentences

Sentences

A **sentence** tells a complete thought about someone or something. It begins with a capital letter and ends with a period (.).

Example: The children are having fun.

A. Check ✔ if the words make a sentence. Cross ✘ if they do not.

1. The monkeys are playing in the tree. ☐

2. There is a bridge that. ☐

3. I want a cup of. ☐

4. The baby is crying. ☐

5. The dog is hungry. ☐

6. The fountain in the centre of the mall. ☐

7. We play badminton every Sunday. ☐

8. She never likes. ☐

126 Complete EnglishSmart · *Grade 2*

Subjects

A sentence has two main parts – a subject and a predicate.

The **subject** tells whom or what the sentence is about.

Example: <u>Dad</u> puts a star at the top of the Christmas tree.

B. Circle the subject of each sentence.

1. Mrs. Maddison holds a party for Brad's birthday.

2. Brad's father puts six candles on the cake.

3. The children are wearing party hats.

4. Brad is making a wish.

5. Nina has a flower on her T-shirt.

6. The birthday cake is big.

7. They have fun at the party.

8. Andy wins the game.

9. Brad's parents give him a bike as a present.

10. The party ends around five.

Predicates

The **predicate** is the part of a sentence that tells what the subject is or what the subject does.

Example: We <u>like going to the beach in summer</u>.

C. Underline the predicate of each sentence.

1. We <u>can go cherry-picking in July</u>.

2. "The First Noel" <u>is a Christmas carol</u>.

3. My brother <u>is working on his Science project</u>.

4. The shops <u>are closed on New Year's Day</u>.

5. You <u>need a stick to play hockey</u>.

6. The children <u>have pizza for lunch</u>.

7. The bus stop <u>is in front of the park</u>.

8. Rita <u>is wearing a pink skirt</u>.

9. Kevin <u>is sick today</u>.

10. The mother bird <u>is feeding her babies</u>.

11. The baby birds <u>like eating worms</u>.

D. Draw lines to match the subjects with the predicates to form sentences.

1. My dad •
2. The birds •
3. The book •
4. The stars •
5. My cat •

   A is about animals of the jungle.

   B looks like a tiger.

   C works in a coffee shop.

   D are twinkling in the sky.

   E are in the nest.

E. Look at each picture. Write a predicate to complete the sentence.

1. The Parliament Buildings _____ .

2. The dog _____ .

3. Howard _____ .

> **Telling Sentences and Imperative Sentences**
>
> A **telling sentence** tells about someone or something. An **imperative sentence** tells someone to do something. Both types of sentences begin with a capital letter and end with a period (.).
>
> *Examples:* A bicycle has two wheels. (telling)
> Park your bicycle there. (imperative)

A. Colour ⓣ if it is a telling sentence. Colour ⓘ if it is an imperative sentence.

1. Tell me the truth.

2. Curry is hot.

3. Never ever give up.

4. This is an ice cream parlour.

5. Shh! Don't make any noise.

6. Plants need sunlight and water.

B. Write the telling sentences correctly. Begin with a capital letter and end with a period.

1. it snows in winter

   _____

2. they are sitting at the table

   _____

3. this is made of glass

   _____

4. the news is on at nine

   _____

   _____

C. Rewrite the following as imperative sentences.

1. Could you turn down the volume of the TV?

   _____

2. You shouldn't shout at others.

   _____

3. Can you tell me the truth?

   _____

4. You have to write your name on the front page.

   _____

Asking Sentences and Exclamatory Sentences

An **asking sentence** asks about someone or something. It begins with a capital letter and ends with a question mark (?).

Example: What do you want for dinner?

An **exclamatory sentence** shows a strong emotion like fear, anger, or excitement. It begins with a capital letter and ends with an exclamation mark (!).

Example: Oh, the house is on fire!

D. **Put "?" or "!" at the end of each sentence. Write "A" for an asking sentence or "E" for an exclamatory sentence.**

1. Oh no, I forgot my key

2. You look great

3. Isn't that amazing

4. How lovely these flowers are

5. Is that what you want

6. How can I stop this

7. What a gorgeous view

8. What's that in your hand

9. The fireworks are awesome

E. Read the answers and write the asking sentences. Use the given words to begin the asking sentences.

1. _____

   Mother's Day is in May. (When)

2. _____

   We can put some eggs in the salad. (What)

3. _____

   I'm seven. (How old)

4. _____

   It's under the chair. (Where)

F. Write an exclamatory sentence for each situation.

1. Your friend came first in a race.

   _____

2. You just dropped your mom's favourite vase.

   _____

3. Your friend is showing you his collection of robots.

   _____

4. You just bumped into a friend on the street.

   _____

Punctuation

All sentences end with punctuation marks.
- A telling sentence or an imperative sentence ends with a period (.).
  Examples: She is my friend.
  Line up, children.

- An asking sentence ends with a question mark (?).
  Example: What's going on here?

- An exclamatory sentence ends with an exclamation mark (!).
  Example: It sounds brilliant!

A. Check ✔ if the sentence ends with the correct punctuation. Put the correct punctuation on the line if it is wrong.

1. We ran the race last Friday!   _____

2. How many of you joined the race!   _____

3. What an exciting race?   _____

4. Who won at last.   _____

5. How lucky he is!   _____

6. Never run right after lunch.   _____

B. Fill in the missing punctuation marks.

Have you ever watched the movie *Men in Black* (1) If you have, you probably remember Frank – the dog providing information to the MIB (2) Did you know that the movie actually brought about a craze of keeping pugs in many countries around the world (3)

Pugs have big eyes on their wrinkly faces (4) Their stocky build makes them look a bit fierce, but if you have kept a pug before, you know how friendly and sociable it is (5) Pugs are playful and obedient, so they make good company (6)

If you still don't have any idea of what pugs are like, borrow the video of *Men in Black* from your friends or from the local library (7) You'll discover how amazing Frank the Pug is (8) You might want to keep a pug after watching the movie too (9)

Capitalization

All sentences begin with capital letters. All proper nouns begin with capital letters too. Names of people, pets, places, days, months, festivals, and titles of books, songs, and movies are all proper nouns.

Example: Jamie and I watched "The Lion King" at the Princess of Wales Theatre.

C. Rewrite the titles below with proper capitalization.

1. beauty and the beast

2. anne of green gables

Don't capitalize articles and prepositions if they are not the first word in a title.

3. the prince and the pauper

4. the emperor's new clothes

5. goldilocks and the three bears

6. the water horse: legend of the deep

D. Rewrite the sentences with proper capitalization.

> Always use capital for "I" when referring to yourself.

1. i went trick-or-treating with my friends on halloween night.

   _____

   _____

   _____

2. it was a friday.

   _____

3. jennifer dressed up as a witch.

   _____

4. ryan wanted a "spiderman" costume.

   _____

   _____

5. my neighbour, mrs. jevon, gave us lots of treats.

   _____

   _____

6. jennifer, ryan, and i then enjoyed our treats together.

   _____

   _____

Word Order

Sentences need to make sense. The order of the words in a sentence can change the meaning of the sentence.

Example: The man drove the car.
The car drove the man.

A. **Look at each picture. Check ✔ the sentence that tells about it.**

1. The bird is pointing at the girl. ◯

   The girl is pointing at the bird. ◯

2. The beaver is building a dam. ◯

   The dam is building a beaver. ◯

3. The plate is on the hamburger. ◯

   The hamburger is on the plate. ◯

4. The lion is chasing the rat. ◯

   The rat is chasing the lion. ◯

B. Look at the picture. Put the words in order to make sentences.

1. at   children   campsite   the   are   a

_____

2. putting   a   tent   they   up   are

_____

3. they   tent   very   a   have   big

_____

4. their   grass   on   put   they   backpacks   the

_____

5. Norman   a   raccoon   sees

_____

6. for   is   food   looking   it

_____

7. bear   is   behind   tree   there   a   the

_____

Related Sentences

We put sentences that are related together. They should be about the same topic.

Example: It's raining heavily. We can't go out and play. We hope that the rain will stop very soon.

C. **Read each group of sentences. Put a line through the one that does not belong.**

1. Our puppy is cute. She likes playing with us. The children are in the backyard.

2. Jane is the youngest in her family. Kate lives next to Jane. The two girls walk to school together every day.

3. I love ice cream. It is a sunny day. It is the best summer treat. Which flavour do you like?

4. The fishermen's boat is big. My dad likes fishing. He goes fishing on weekends.

5. Rachael's birthday is on Saturday. Sunday is the first day of the week. She has invited us to her party.

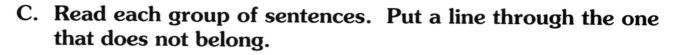

Sequencing

Sentences should be put in a logical order so that people can follow the idea.

Example: It is facing the lake. My parents have a cottage in Muskoka. We spend our summer there every year. (✗)

My parents have a cottage in Muskoka. It is facing the lake. We spend our summer there every year. (✔)

D. Put each group of sentences in the correct order. Write 1, 2, 3, and 4 on the lines.

1. ___ I played computer games after lunch.

   ___ I helped Mom set the table for dinner.

   ___ I had ham and eggs for breakfast.

   ___ I got up early this morning.

2. ___ But she thinks chocolate ice cream is the best of all.

   ___ She likes chocolate cake.

   ___ Heidi likes all kinds of chocolate treats.

   ___ She likes chocolate mousse too.

Be – Present Form

Use "am/is/are not" to tell about a present state.

Example: The boots <u>are not</u> new.

Use "am/is/are not" and the "ing" form of a verb to tell about what is not going on.

Example: Cedric <u>is not walking</u> to school.

A. Circle the correct words and choose the correct ending for each sentence.

- singing in the nest
- my neighbour
- functioning well
- a girl
- twins

1. My sister and I | am not | is not | are not | _____ .

2. Shelley | am not | is not | are not | _____ .

3. I | am not | is not | are not | _____ .

4. The machines are old. They | am not | is not | are not |

_____ .

5. The mother bird | am not | is not | are not | _____

_____ .

Be – Past Form

Use "was/were not" to tell about a past state.

Example: My parents <u>were not</u> at home when all the lights went out.

Use "was/were not" and the "ing" form of a verb to tell what was not going on at a past time.

Example: He <u>was not driving</u> when the accident happened.

B. Complete the sentences with the correct form of "be" and "not".

1. The girl _____ playing when I saw her.

2. Rachel and Persy _____ classmates last year.

3. I _____ waiting for the bus at two o'clock yesterday.

4. We _____ looking when the clown came out.

C. Rewrite the sentences as negative.

1. They were singing when the bell rang.

_____

_____

2. Sue was at home when Jane called.

_____

Other Verbs – Present Form

For a singular subject except "I" and "you", add "does not" before the base form of the verb to talk about the present.

Example: She <u>does not live</u> near her school.

For a plural subject, "I", and "you", add "do not" before the base form.

Example: Penguins <u>do not fly</u>.

D. Change the verbs to negative.

	I	Macy	Ann and Roy
swim	do not swim		
dance			
join			
drink			

E. Rewrite the sentences as negative.

1. Jamie likes playing baseball.

_____

2. I go fishing with my dad.

_____

3. Mr. and Mrs. Moore want to live in the city.

_____

Other Verbs – Past Form

For all subjects, add "did not" before the base form of the verb to talk about the past.

Example: They <u>did not watch</u> yesterday's game.

F. The underlined words are wrong. Write the correct words in the boxes.

1. The children <u>did not played</u> in the pool yesterday.

2. Dad <u>does not go</u> to work last week.

3. I <u>do not visits</u> my grandparents last Christmas.

4. I <u>did not studying</u> in this school last year.

G. Put the words in order to form negative sentences.

1. video games   did   yesterday   Jason   play   not

   _____

   _____

2. come   I   race   not   in   first   did   the

   _____

Synonyms, Antonyms, and Homonyms

Synonyms

Synonyms are words that mean the same.

Examples: order – command
inspect – examine
tiny – small

A. Draw lines to join the synonyms.

1. answer •
2. clever •
3. wrong •
4. fix •
5. make •
6. stop •
7. change •
8. funny •

• repair
• solution
• humorous
• incorrect
• smart
• build
• alter
• halt

Antonyms

Antonyms are words that mean the opposite.

Examples: dark – bright
              first – last
              cold – hot

B. Put each word in the box with its antonym.

stay

sad

slow

easy

wrong

depart   go
correct   glad
swift   right
difficult   fast
happy   hard
speedy   leave
proper   jolly
challenging

Homonyms

Homonyms are words that have the same sound but different spellings and meanings.

Examples: fair – fare
not – knot
horse – hoarse

C. Circle the homonyms in each group of words.

You have to circle two or three words in each group.

1. oar   or   ore   owl

2. tall   tale   tail   tile

3. hire   heir   hare   hair

4. blue   blow   blew   boo

5. sow   saw   sew   so

6. two   tow   toe   toll

7. sent   scent   saint   cent

D. Complete the crossword puzzle with synonyms (S), antonyms (A), or homonyms (H) of the clue words.

Across

A. rabbit (S)

B. deep (A)

C. strange (S)

D. destroy (A)

E. close (S)

Down

1. paws (H)
2. aloud (H)
3. wait (H)
4. always (A)

A. Fill in the blanks with the correct prepositions.

1._____ the afternoon 2._____ the
   In / On   in / on

day they retrieved the colour blue, Lilian, Ned,

and Wilkin came to a meadow. There were lots

of flowers 3._____ the grass. "Do you know the colour
              in / on

of the flowers, Wilkin?" asked Lilian eagerly. "Sorry, Lilian.

I've never seen these flowers before. They could be

any colours."

The children moved on. 4._____ dusk, they saw
                            At / In

a tree 5._____ the top of a knoll. There was an apple
          at / by

6._____ the tree. Ned was thrilled. He shouted,
   over / in

"Look! We've found the colour red!" He ran over to the

tree at once.

"Wait, Ned!" Wilkin stopped him. "It may also be

green or golden. We'd better try something else." Then

Lilian cried out, "Look at that animal 7._____ the tree.
                                          under / between

Do you know its colour, Wilkin?" "Lilian, that's a skunk.

All skunks are black and white in colour!"

B. Match the subjects with the predicates to form sentences. Write the letters in the boxes.

A had been retrieved.

B is impossible for us to get this wrong.

C is always brown.

D was back!

E were delighted.

F can tell the colour of the tree trunk.

G said the magic words, "Retrieve colour!"

H put his hand on the tree trunk and said, "Brown!"

1. But wait, we ☐

2. The trunk of an apple tree ☐

3. It ☐

4. All three of them ☐

5. Ned ☐

6. Then Lilian ☐

7. The colour brown ☐

8. So, two colours ☐

C. Correct the words that need capitalization and put proper punctuation at the end of the sentences. Then write the sentence numbers in the correct places.

1. can we do the same with the leaves

2. no, we can't

3. leaves are not always green

4. they change colours in fall and winter

5. don't you know it's summer now

6. lilian, touch the leaves and say the colour

7. ned, say the magic words

8. great, the colour green is back

Types of Sentences

Telling	Imperative	Asking	Exclamatory

D. Put the words in order to make sentences.

1. came another children tree to the .

_____

2. in many there fruits the were tree .

_____

3. they or oranges are grapefruits ?

_____

4. we should "orange" say "yellow" or ?

_____

5. we one of can them eat .

_____

6. found orange they that it out was tree an .

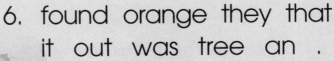

_____

_____

7. retrieved the they colour orange .

_____

_____

E. Write 1 to 6 on the lines to put the sentences in the correct order.

___ To play safe, the children sat there for almost two hours staring at the flowers.

___ The next day, the children came across some very tall flowers.

___ That was how the colour yellow was retrieved.

___ Wilkin thought they were sunflowers.

___ He told Lilian and Ned that sunflowers were yellow in colour, and they always faced the sun.

___ They really rotated to face the sun!

F. Change the given words to negative using "not".

1. The children were happy to see that the things around them _____ simply in black and
   were
   white now.

2. It _____ to find the remaining colours.
   was difficult

3. They _____ far from the end of the quest.
   were

4. The children _____ to waste any time.
   wanted

G. Fill in the blanks with the synonyms (S), antonyms (A), or homonyms (H) of the given words.

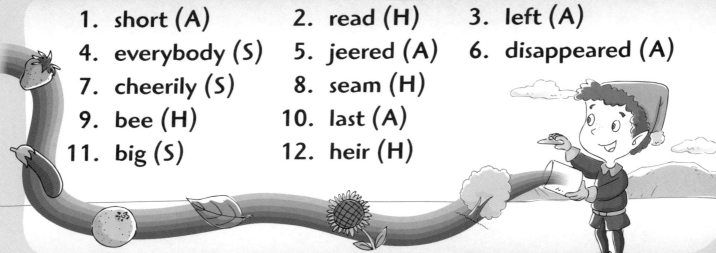

1. short (A)
2. read (H)
3. left (A)
4. everybody (S)
5. jeered (A)
6. disappeared (A)
7. cheerily (S)
8. seam (H)
9. bee (H)
10. last (A)
11. big (S)
12. heir (H)

Before 1._____ , the children retrieved the colour 2._____ with a strawberry and the colour purple with an eggplant. They 3._____ to Colourland.

4._____ in Colourland was waiting for them at the gate. They 5._____ and welcomed the three children.

Coby the Elf suddenly 6._____ with a pop. He laughed 7._____ and said, "This didn't 8._____ to 9._____ a challenge for you. I'd better think of something more challenging 10._____ time. It's going to be 11._____ fun."

Then he disappeared into the 12._____ .

1 The Five Senses

Human beings have five senses: touch, smell, sight, hearing, and taste. We touch with our hands. The human hand has many bones. We smell with our nose and see with our eyes. We hear with our ears and taste with our tongue.

A.   Write three words that match each sense.

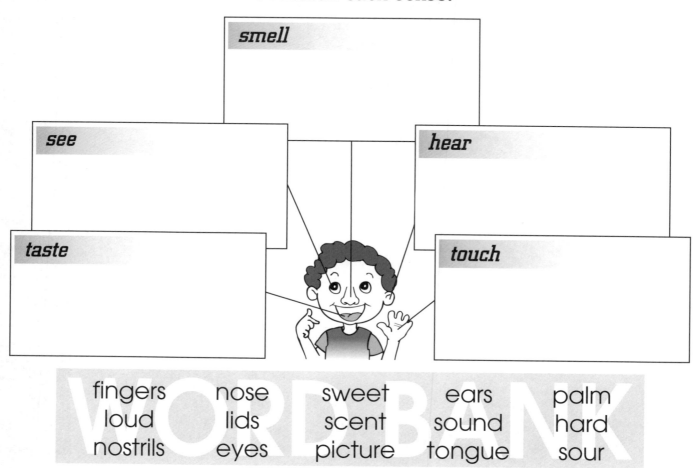

smell

see

hear

taste

touch

WORD BANK

fingers   nose   sweet   ears   palm
loud   lids   scent   sound   hard
nostrils   eyes   picture   tongue   sour

B. Fill in the missing letters to complete the words.

1. h __ m __ n
2. s __ e __ __
3. h __ __ r __ __ g
4. b __ __ __ s
5. h __ __ d
6. h __ __ r
7. t __ __ t __
8. t __ __ __ h

C. Draw a line to match each pair of words that rhyme.

Words that rhyme sound the same at the end.

1. bone •

2. five •

3. sense •

4. hear •

5. nose •

6. eye •

7. smell •

8. see •

• tell

• ear

• spy

• tense

• cone

• rose

• bee

• hive

D. Unscramble the letters on the hands and write the words they make.

1.

_____

2.

_____

3.

_____

4.

_____

5.

_____

6.

_____

7.

_____

8.

_____

9.

_____

10.

_____

11.

_____

12.

_____

E. Find the words in the word search.

k	y	d	m	s	c	u	s	i	g	h	t	b	z
x	w	t	u	g	k	m	h	e	o	d	f	h	i
b	d	o	f	j	e	c	o	k	h	q	t	s	u
p	w	n	r	v	a	f	t	o	u	c	h	w	o
d	k	g	k	u	r	i	w	y	m	b	p	v	l
a	z	u	h	l	s	q	b	g	a	o	o	m	h
s	e	e	c	p	x	u	h	a	n	d	t	f	e
y	i	t	f	v	j	a	o	l	u	y	d	x	a
g	p	s	m	e	l	l	w	q	c	j	m	i	r
k	m	o	r	y	o	y	b	i	g	b	v	l	c
t	a	s	t	e	r	t	o	z	r	o	n	r	q
h	c	u	w	s	j	v	n	o	s	e	h	m	k
w	i	p	s	e	n	s	e	b	l	f	i	v	e
n	l	b	c	r	b	f	s	h	x	p	d	t	i

Word Bank

human	five	smell	bones
tongue	hand	touch	taste
nose	hear	sight	sense
see	eyes	ears	body

2 Changing Seasons

There are four seasons in every year: Spring, Summer, Fall, and Winter.

Spring is the season when the weather gets warmer and buds come out on trees. Spring begins in March and ends in June.

Summer begins in June and ends in September. It is the season when temperatures get high. The leaves are green and the grass is too!

Fall is the season when leaves change from green to orange, yellow, red, and brown. Leaves change colour because the temperature drops.

Winter starts in December and ends in March. In Canada, there is usually a lot of snow in winter. Snow is one type of precipitation.

A. Look at the boxes. Finish the words that belong to each season.

SPRING

w __ __ m __ __

b __ __ s

M __ __ c __

SUMMER

A __ g __ s __

h __ t

__ __ n

FALL

o _ _ _ _ e

y _ _ _ _ w

_ _ _ _ n

WINTER

s _ _ _

D _ _ _ m _ _ _

pr_ _ _ _ _ _ _ t_ _ _

B. Join the pictures to the words.

snow

leaves

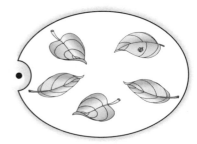

Winter

Fall

hot

Spring

Summer

buds

Word Families – Rhyming Words

C. Fill in the missing letters to make words that rhyme.

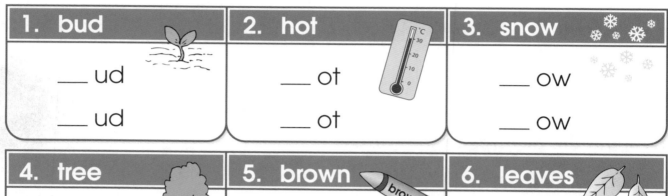

1. bud	2. hot	3. snow
___ ud	___ ot	___ ow
___ ud	___ ot	___ ow

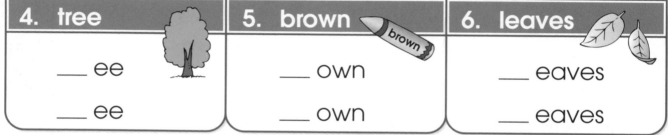

4. tree	5. brown	6. leaves
___ ee	___ own	___ eaves
___ ee	___ own	___ eaves

D. The words in these leaves are scrambled. Sort them and write each on the line below.

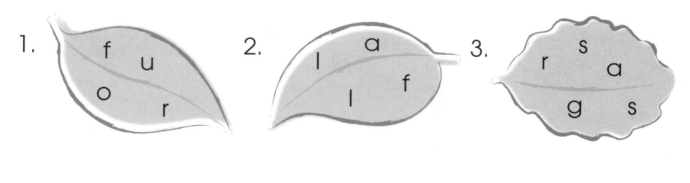

1. f u o r

2. a l f l

3. s r a g s

4. w o n s

5. a r e y

6. b w r n o

_____

_____

_____

7.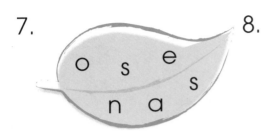

8.

9.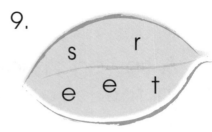

_____ _____ _____

E. Put the words in order and write the correct sentences.

1. | leaves | The | green | are |

_____

2. | colours | Leaves | many | in | are |

_____

3. | four | There | seasons | year | every | in | are |

_____

4. | begins | March | Spring | ends | June | in | and | in |

_____

5. | Snow | precipitation | is | a | of | type |

_____

6. | season | Each | is | three | months | about | long |

_____

3 The Butterfly

A tiny egg is laid on a leaf. Then the egg hatches and becomes a caterpillar. The caterpillar eats and eats and becomes very fat. It forms a cover around itself and becomes a pupa.

After a few weeks, the pupa hatches and a butterfly is born. The female butterfly is not as colourful as the male.

The butterfly flies among flowers and eats nectar. Sometimes it feeds on the juices from fruits that are rotting.

A. Look at each picture. Write what it is.

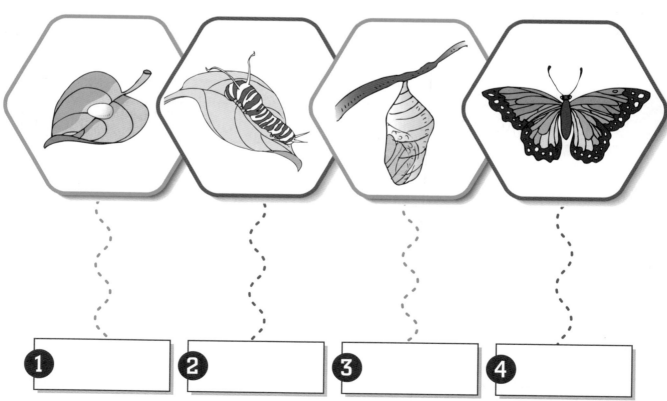

1
2
3
4

B. Draw lines to match the butterflies with the flowers to form words.

1 fe
2 pu
3 butter
4 nec
5 colour

tar
pa
male
fly
ful

C. Read the first word in each box. Write letters in the blanks to make new words.

1. **laid**

   ___ aid

   ___ aid

2. **fat**

   ___ at

   ___ at

3. **few**

   ___ ew

   ___ ew

4. **born**

   ___ orn

   ___ orn

5. **male**

   ___ ale

   ___ ale

6. **not**

   ___ ot

   ___ ot

D. Read each sentence. Write a word for each picture.

WORD BANK

egg   caterpillar   butterfly   fruits

leaf   pupa   flowers

A tiny **1** ⬭ is laid on a **2** 🍃 .

The egg hatches and becomes a **3** 🐛 .

The caterpillar becomes a **4** 🦋 .

The pupa hatches and a **5** 🦋 is born.

The butterfly eats nectar from **6** 🌸 .

It also eats juices from **7** 🍓 .

1. __ __ __   2. __ __ __ __

3. __ __ __ __ __ __ __ __ __ __ __

4. __ __ __ __   5. __ __ __ __ __ __ __ __ __

6. __ __ __ __ __ __   7. __ __ __ __ __ __

E. Read the word. Write it in a sentence. The first one is done for you.

1. tiny

   The eggs are tiny.

2. laid

   _____

3. leaf

   _____

4. caterpillar

   _____

5. pupa

   _____

6. butterfly

   _____

7. fruit

   _____

4 Crispy Squares

Amanda and her mom are making crispy squares. Maybe you would like their recipe.

Ingredients:

- 5 cups of rice crispies
- 1 packet of small marshmallows
- $\frac{1}{2}$ cup of margarine

Utensils:

- 1 large bowl
- 1 saucepan
- 1 spatula
- 1 large glass baking dish
- measuring spoons

Directions :

Melt margarine in saucepan. Pour in marshmallows slowly and keep stirring until marshmallows are melted. Take marshmallow mixture from stove. Mix in large bowl with rice crispies.

Pat into large, greased baking dish. Cool in refrigerator. Cut into squares.

A. Read the letters inside each crispy square. Unscramble to make a word.

1
erci

2
blwo

3
spuc

4
ciyrsp

5
orpu

6
toevs

7
noosps

8
kabing

9
hisd

10
qussera

11
napseacu

12
retxium

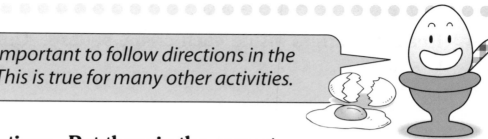

In baking, it is important to follow directions in the correct order. This is true for many other activities.

B. Read these directions. Put them in the correct order.

ⓐ Mix eggs and milk together.
Take the ingredients out of the fridge.
Pour pancake batter onto a frying pan.
Pour in flour and baking powder.

1. _____

2. _____

3. _____

4. _____

ⓑ Blow up the balloon.
Twist the opening to make a knot.
Take a balloon out of the package.
Buy a package of balloons.

1. _____

2. _____

3. _____

4. _____

C. Look at each picture. Write a sentence about what is happening.

1

_____

_____

_____

_____

2

_____

_____

_____

_____

3

_____

_____

_____

_____

4

_____

_____

_____

_____

5 Nunavut

Nunavut is a large territory in the north of Canada. It is near the North Pole. It is very cold there. Not many plants grow there because it is so cold.

In Nunavut, there are six months of darkness and six months of daylight. You might see the sun shining at 9 o'clock at night in June.

Would you like to go to bed when the sun is shining and go to school when it is dark outside?

A. **Read the sentences. Find the missing words from the passage.**

The last two are for you to figure out.

1. Nunavut is a _____ in Canada.

2. Nunavut is near the _____ _____ .

3. In Nunavut, there are _____ months of darkness.

4. The sun might be shining at _____ in June.

5. Not many _____ grow in Nunavut.

6. Plants don't grow because it is very _____ .

7. In the cold weather, people wear warm _____ .

8. Some people in Nunavut ride on _____ .

B. **Sort out the letters in the igloos to make new words.**

1.
   a n
   a d
   a c

   _____

2.
   m h
   s o
   t n

   _____

3.
   o d
   c
   l

   _____

4.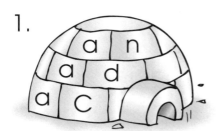
   d
   e
   b

   _____

5.
   o l
   o c
   s h

   _____

6.
   k
   r a
   d

   _____

7.
   h g
   n t
   i

   _____

8.
   n h
   o r
   t

   _____

9.
   g l
   a e
   r

   _____

10.
    g
    w o
    r

    _____

11.
    p t
    a s
    n l

    _____

12.
    a e
    r
    n

    _____

Sometimes you can find smaller words inside large ones.

NORTH

C. Read each word. Find the smaller word and write it on the lines below. The first one is done for you.

1. north __n__ __o__ __r__	2. Canada __ __ __	3. near __ __ __
4. cold __ __ __	5. there __ __ __	6. not __ __
7. many __ __ __	8. plants __ __ __ __	9. grow __ __ __
10. there __ __ __	11. darkness __ __ __	12. daylight __ __ __
13. daylight __ __ __	14. outside __ __ __	15. outside __ __ __

Challenge

Try one of your own!

_____ (large word)

_____ (small word)

D. Use these words in sentences.

1. large

_____

_____

 2. north

_____

_____

3. cold

_____

_____

 4. plants

_____

_____

5. months

_____

_____

 6. school

_____

_____

7. dark

_____

_____

6 Word Fun

Poetry – Alphabet Rhymes

A is for apple.

B is for <u>bog</u>.

C is for cat and

D is for <u>dog</u>.

E is for egg.

F is for <u>fat</u>.

G is for game and

H is for <u>hat</u>.

Did you notice that the last words in the second and fourth lines rhyme or sound the same at the end?

A. Make up an alphabet rhyme of your own. Fill in the blanks with rhyming words.

I is for icicle.

J is for 1. _____ .

K is for kite and

L is for 3. _____ .

M is for moose.

N is for 2. _____ .

O is for otter and

P is for 4. _____ .

B. **Read the clues and complete the word puzzle.**

Across
A. An animal that lives in water and rhymes with "potter"
B. It slithers and rhymes with "cake".
C. This animal is afraid of cats but rhymes with "cat".
D. A fat animal that rhymes with "wig"

Down
1. A woolly animal that rhymes with "deep"
2. A huge sea animal that rhymes with "tale"
3. An animal that rhymes with "goose"
4. A big cat with stripes
5. A big animal that rhymes with "pear"
6. A frog-like animal that rhymes with "road"

C. **Write a word that sounds the same as the underlined word in each sentence.**

1. The <u>ad</u> was for chocolate chip cookies.

    Can you _____ 35 and 23?

2. The trees are <u>bare</u> in winter.

    The _____ climbed the tree.

3. The wind <u>blew</u> over the water.

    The water and sky are _____ .

4. Emily walked <u>by</u> the house.

    She wants to _____ a new dress.

5. <u>I</u> hope to go to the city.

    Did you hurt your _____ ?

6. Mom likes the <u>red</u> roses.

    I _____ a funny story last night.

7. Mom used the <u>flour</u> to make cookies.

    I picked a _____ to give
    to my mom.

Acrostic Poetry

Acrostic poems have one word that goes ↓ . Each letter is the first letter of a new word. All the words might belong to the first word in some way.

Curl
Animal
Tabby

D. Use these words to write acrostic poems.

1. **D** _____
   O _____
   G _____

2. **H** _____
   A _____
   T _____

3. **B** _____
   A _____
   L _____
   L _____

E. Using words you like, write an acrostic poem of your own. Draw a picture to go with it.

7 What Makes a Fish a Fish?

Fish live in ponds, streams, lakes, and oceans. Some fish are kept as pets in fishbowls and aquariums.

Fish swim by moving their tails and waving their fins.

All fish have backbones. Most fish have skin that is covered with scales. Scales protect the skin from cuts and scrapes. There is slime over the scales to protect the fish from germs in the water.

Fish have gills for breathing. Most fish eat tiny plants or tiny animals like worms.

Word Family – Rhyming Words

A. Look at each word. Fill in the letters that make rhyming words.

1. fin
   ___ in
   ___ in

2. pet
   ___ et
   ___ et

3. gill
   ___ ill
   ___ ill

4. tail
   ___ ail
   ___ ail

5. fish
   ___ ish
   ___ ish

6. lake
   ___ ake
   ___ ake

B. Each of these sentences has a word that is not spelled correctly. Cross out the word and write the correct spelling in the box. Use the word bank to help you.

there   eat   oceans   wave
scales   streams   tails   aquariums

1. Codfish live in oseans.

2. All fish have backbones and tales.

3. Most fish also have scails.

4. Fish waive their fins to help them swim.

5. Most fish eet tiny plants.

6. Their are many species of fish.

7. Some fish live in steams.

8. Some fish are kept in aguariums.

C. **The words on the fish are jumbled. Sort them out and write them as sentences.**

1. live   oceans   Fish   and   in   ponds   .

_____

2. swim   moving   Fish   by   tails   .   their

_____

3. fish   All   backbones   have   .

_____

4. help   .   Gills   to   fish   breathe

_____

5. protect   Scales   fish's   the   skin   .

_____

6. make   pets   .   Some   good   fish

_____

D. Make a sentence with each of these words.

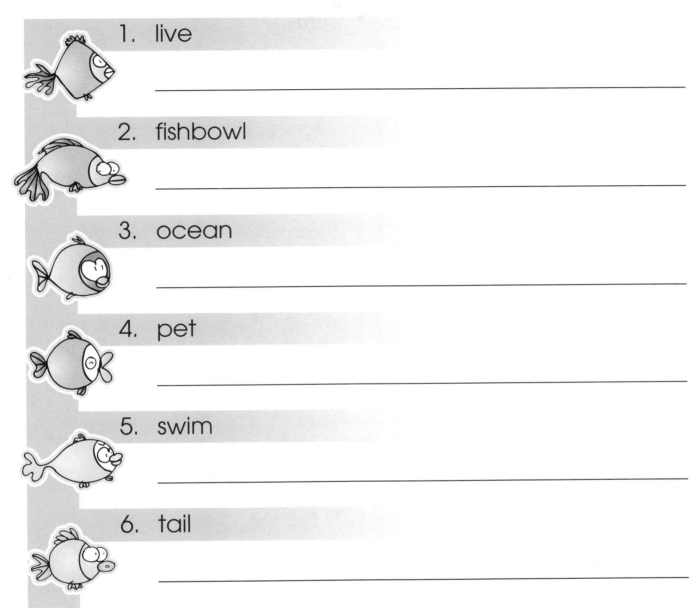

1. live

_____

2. fishbowl

_____

3. ocean

_____

4. pet

_____

5. swim

_____

6. tail

_____

 Challenge

 scales

skin

Use these two words to write a sentence.

_____

_____

A. Unscramble the letters to make words.

1 x b o

_____

2 p c u

_____

3 c s k o

_____

4 t a b

_____

5 c e k a

_____

6 k i l m

_____

7 s e g o o

_____

8 p a m l

_____

9 l f e a

_____

10 s l a c e s

_____

11 i s n c e t

_____

12 l l i g

_____

B. Find the small word hidden inside each of these larger words.

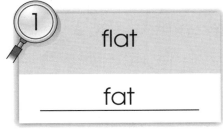

1 flat

_____ fat _____

2 stop

_____

3 spot

_____

4 tart

_____

5 pear

_____

6 treat

_____

7 witch

_____

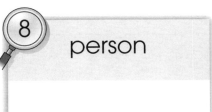

8 person

_____

9 summer

_____

10 cold

_____

11 sand

_____

12 fish

_____

13 tray

_____

14 season

_____

15 four

_____

16 cookie

_____

17 warm

_____

18 plant

_____

C. Put the words in the correct order to make sentences.

> *Don't forget to begin a sentence with a capital letter and put a period at the end of it.*

1. computer plays Mike his with

_____

2. Amanda pool in swims her

_____

3. are there books four table on the

_____

4. the today is sun hot

_____

5. Caitlin shoes red has of a pair

_____

6. dark bats look food in the for

_____

D. Read each sentence. Fill in the blank with a verb that makes sense.

driving licking riding sucking

skates plays paints

danced watered cut

1. Cathy _____ at the arena.

2. Bill _____ the room green.

3. Is your dad _____ you to school?

4. How many girls are _____ their bikes?

5. Jason _____ baseball well.

6. The cat is _____ her paw.

7. Janet _____ the plants yesterday.

8. The baby boy is _____ his thumb.

9. Clare _____ the apple in half.

10. We _____ to the music.

E. Each sentence below has a word that sounds right but is not spelled correctly. Cross out the wrong word and write the correct one on the line below.

| mail | ate | played | made | sail |
| trade | too | flower | | |

1. The boat set sale on the lake.

   _____

2. Rob plaid games with his friends.

   _____

3. She maid a new recipe.

   _____

4. Did you trayed the hockey card?

   _____

5. Tom eight his lunch quickly.

   _____

6. The letter arrived with the male.

   _____

7. I want to go two.

   _____

8. This flour is beautiful.

   _____

F. The first word in each set is given. Find letters that will make the words in that set.

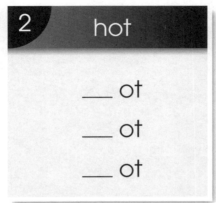

1 laid

___ aid

___ aid

___ aid

2 hot

___ ot

___ ot

___ ot

3 four

___ our

___ our

___ our

4 male

___ ale

___ ale

___ ale

5 nap

___ ap

___ ap

___ ap

6 fin

___ in

___ in

___ in

7 pet

___ et

___ et

___ et

8 all

___ ll

___ ll

___ ll

9 gill

___ ill

___ ill

___ ill

10 lake

___ ake

___ ake

___ ake

11 bail

___ ail

___ ail

___ ail

12 bear

___ ear

___ ear

___ ear

8 Bat Facts

Bats live in almost every country in the world. They do not live in places where it is very hot or very cold.

Bats usually eat fruits or insects. Vampire bats eat the blood of dead birds and cattle.

Bats have good hearing, which helps them to find food. They see best in the dark, which is when they hunt for food.

Bats are useful to farmers because they eat insects and spread seeds.

Noun Hunt

Nouns *tell about people, places, or things.*

A. Find six nouns in "Bat Facts" and write them in the cave.

192   *Complete EnglishSmart* • **Grade 2**

B. Read the clues and complete the word puzzles.

Across	Down
1. You use it to hit the baseball.	A. You wear it on your head.
2. This animal mews.	B. You do this to your pet.
3. It lays on the floor.	C. This small animal has a long tail and sharp teeth.

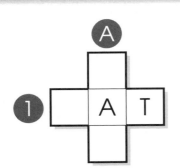 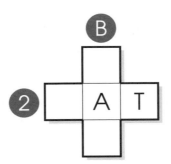 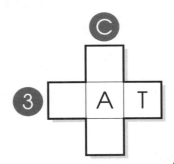

All the words in these 3 puzzles end with "at".

Across	Down
1. Things we eat	A. It has five toes.
2. We use it to build houses.	B. We can see it at night.
3. Midday	C. This is for our head.

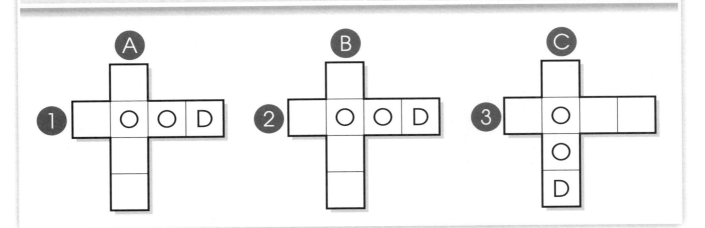

Writing Time

C. Use each of these words in a sentence.

bats   fruit   hearing   seeds

farmers   world   insect   food

Remember that a sentence begins with a capital letter and ends with a period.

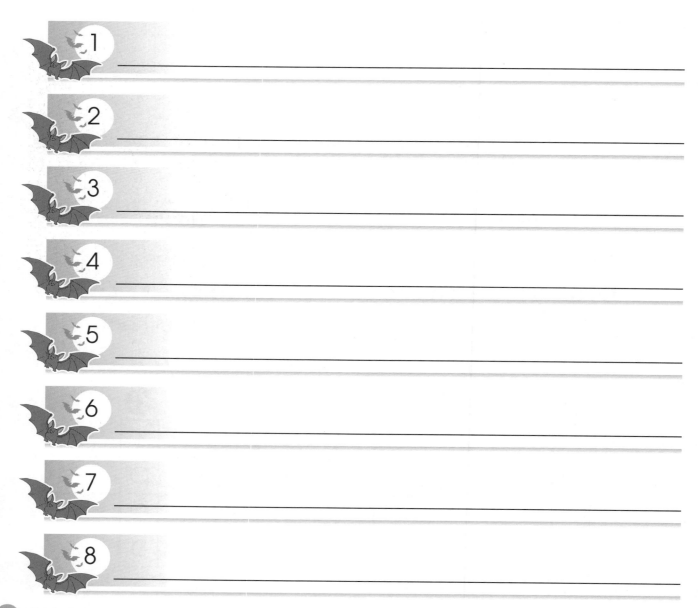

1 _____

2 _____

3 _____

4 _____

5 _____

6 _____

7 _____

8 _____

D. The pictures below are describing the sentences in "Bat Facts". Write a sentence that tells about the picture.

1. _____

   _____

   _____

   _____

2. _____

   _____

   _____

3. _____

   _____

   _____

The Emperor Penguin

The Emperor Penguin is the largest of all penguins. It is about 1.2 metres tall. That's probably taller than you! It has black and grey feathers and yellow ear patches.

The Emperor Penguin lives in the Antarctic. It lives near water, never on dry land. Its food comes from the ocean, mostly fish and krill, which are like shrimp.

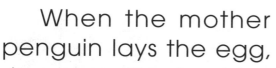

When the mother penguin lays the egg, she goes off to hunt for food. The father Emperor hatches the egg under a flap of skin on top of his feet.

Word Hunt

A. The words below are found in "The Emperor Penguin". Fill in the missing letters.

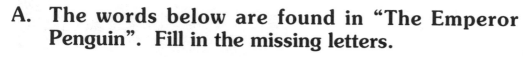

1. p __ __ g __ __ n

2. __ m p __ r __ r

3. A __ t __ __ c __ i __

4. k __ __ __ l

5. h __ __ c h __ s

6. p __ t __ h __ s

7. b __ __ c k

8. y __ l __ o __

9. t __ l l __ r

10. g __ e __

B. **Read the letters on each ice floe. Sort out the letters and write the word.**

1. _____

2. _____

3. _____

4. _____

5. _____

6. _____

C. Sort the words to make sentences.

1. Antarctica . The lives Emperor in Penguin

   _____

2. lives water land . It near dry never on ,

   _____

3. food Penguins their get the from ocean .

   _____

4. for are food Fish penguins krill and .

   _____

5. largest of the The Emperor is penguins .

   _____

6. penguin The hunts food . for mother

   _____

7. father hatches egg The the Emperor .

   _____

D. In each group of sentences, there is one that does not belong. Draw a line through the sentence that does not belong.

Example: The fly flew into the house. It landed on the stove and the table. ~~The tree is near the house.~~

1.

Candy

I love all kinds of candies. Fish is not my favourite food. My favourite candies are gummy bears.

2.

My Bike

I have a new bike. It is red and white. The car goes in the garage. My bike stays in the storage shed.

3.

Amanda's Pool

Amanda loves to swim in her pool. She asks her friends to come for a swim. The flowers grow tall. Her friends like to swim too.

4.

TV Shows

Some of the best TV shows I like are really funny. They make me laugh and laugh. My mom likes to dance.

10 Playing Soccer

Today I started soccer. I went to a big field where there were lots of children the same age as I. They all had the same orange uniforms too!

My soccer coach is named Olivia. She is really nice and friendly. She said, "Hello, my name is Olivia." Then she told us that we would practise twice a week and play games. She said the most important thing was to have fun.

A. Look at the pictures. Write what you think each person is saying.

Hi, my name is Olivia.

1

I like our new coach.

2

B. Read the "describing" words in Column A and draw a line to match each one with a word in Column B.

We wear orange uniforms.

	Column A			Column B
1.	tall	•	•	ladybug
2.	green	•	•	ball
3.	tiny	•	•	knife
4.	blue	•	•	girl
5.	round	•	•	tree
6.	sharp	•	•	grass
7.	pretty	•	•	candy
8.	sweet	•	•	sky
9.	rainy	•	•	game
10.	fun	•	•	day

C. Read each of these sentences. Colour the word that has the same meaning as the underlined word.

big   large

1. I put the <u>small</u> seed in the jar.

| tiny | green |

2. Mike found a <u>giant</u> zucchini in the garden.

| long | huge |

3. Theo kicked the soccer ball <u>two times</u>.

| twice | thrice |

4. There is a very <u>high</u> building in the city.

| big | tall |

5. There were <u>several</u> people waiting.

| a few | many |

6. There were forty <u>thieves</u> in the story.

| robbers | friends |

7. Becca ran <u>quickly</u> to the end of the field.

| fast | slowly |

D. Fill in the blanks with words from the passage.

Today I started 1._____ . I went to

a 2._____ where there were lots of

3._____ . They were the same

4._____ as I. We all had orange

5._____ .

Olivia is our 6._____ . She is nice and

7._____ . She said that we would

8._____ twice a week and play

9._____ . She told us to have

10._____ .

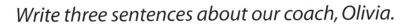

Challenge

Write three sentences about our coach, Olivia.

1. _____

2. _____

3. _____

11 Ladybugs

Ladybugs are insects.
They are often red with black spots.
Some are black with red spots. In
summer, they live on flowers, shrubs,
and in fields. In winter, they live in trees
and houses.

Ladybugs are useful because they eat the insects
that kill plants. These insects are called aphides.
Ladybugs eat over 5,000 aphides in a lifetime.

Ladybugs have some enemies. They are called
parasites and they eat the inside of the ladybug.
Human beings are also their enemies because
they spray them with poison and disturb
their nests and homes.

 **Rhyming Pairs**

Rhyming words *sound the same at the end.*

A. Write a rhyming word to match each word below.

1. nest	___ est	2. spot	___ ot
3. bug	___ ug	4. that	___ at
5. black	___ ack	6. live	___ ive
7. kill	___ ill	8. some	___ ome

B. Draw a line to join each of the words with its meaning.

1. ladybug

2. aphid

3. parasites

4. enemy

5. poison

6. nest

7. disturb

8. shrubs

9. red

10. spots

mess up

a place where birds live

an insect that eats plants and is eaten by ladybugs

a bright colour

a bug that is red and black

low green bushes

someone or something that kills ladybugs

They eat the inside of ladybugs.

a spray to kill insects

dots

C. Draw a line to join each ladybug with a flower to make a word. Write the words on the lines.

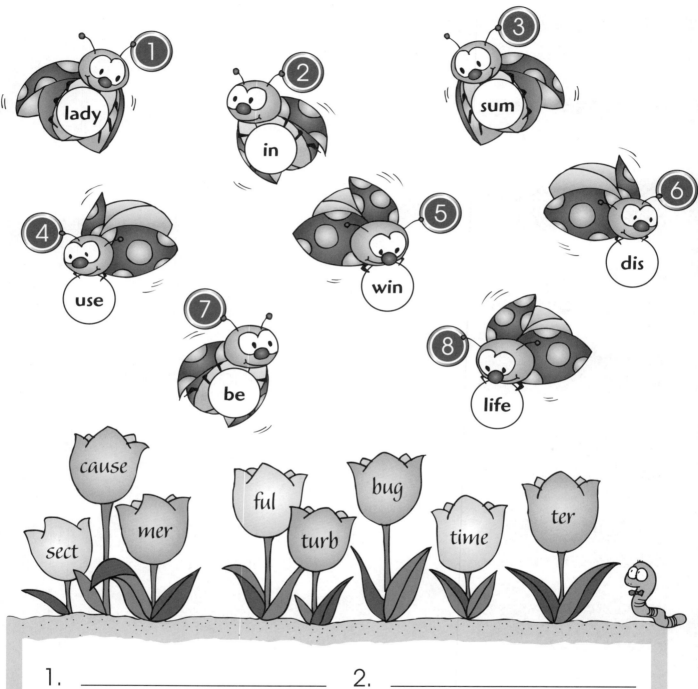

1. _____   2. _____

3. _____   4. _____

5. _____   6. _____

7. _____   8. _____

D. Unscramble the sentences.

> Remember to begin a sentence with a capital letter and put a period at the end of it.

1. are black ladybugs red and

   _____

2. live shrubs they flowers in and

   _____

3. winter they in houses trees and in live

   _____

4. useful are ladybugs eat insects because they

   _____

5. are aphides that insects eat ladybugs

   _____

6. enemies some ladybugs have

   _____

7. are enemies human beings the of ladybugs also

   _____

The New Umbrella

Mom bought me a new umbrella. It is red, blue, and yellow. It looks really neat when you twirl the handle around.

I can use my umbrella in the rain and also in the sun. It protects me from the rain and from getting a sunburn.

My mom told me that the first umbrella was used about 3,000 years ago in Egypt. In more modern times, the first umbrella was used for rain in Scotland in the 1800's.

Making New Words

A. There are smaller words that can come out of larger ones. Find the small word in the larger one.

1. yellow

2. when

3. also

4. rain

5. that

6. told

7. sunburn

8. neat

9. years

10. about

11. more

12. was

B. **Find these words in the word search. Circle the words.**

umbrella   Scotland   years
blue   twirl   time   red   sunburn
neat   yellow   modern   really   handle
protect   Egypt   rain   new

e	r	t	y	a	j	m	r	y	u	d	e	m	v	t	y
c	n	k	i	g	r	n	o	e	f	i	S	e	d	e	w
t	i	u	m	b	r	e	l	l	a	e	c	l	o	f	g
w	a	n	E	y	e	w	o	l	y	m	o	d	e	r	n
p	l	i	g	a	d	m	n	o	w	a	t	f	a	r	d
h	S	o	q	r	b	o	t	w	i	r	l	d	E	o	r
l	a	z	s	q	u	i	b	r	h	i	a	e	x	p	m
d	l	o	u	w	b	q	u	v	o	p	n	m	s	q	y
w	h	a	n	d	l	e	r	m	E	f	d	b	e	u	o
y	n	i	b	w	u	w	i	i	g	r	n	a	s	x	u
e	d	t	u	r	e	a	l	l	y	w	e	d	r	j	E
a	m	t	r	u	m	b	p	w	p	t	d	w	i	o	n
r	a	i	n	s	d	p	r	o	t	e	c	t	o	y	b
s	k	m	u	d	e	a	b	s	e	m	b	i	v	f	w
y	n	e	a	t	r	w	a	e	k	i	u	t	a	S	b

C. Put the words in the correct order to make sentences.

> *Always begin a sentence with a capital letter and put a period at the end of it.*

1. is   new   umbrella   my   colourful

_____

2. umbrella   not   big   too   my   is

_____

3. fun   is   it   twirl   the   umbrella   to

_____

4. first   umbrella   the   Egypt   in   used   was

_____

5. protects   me   the   umbrella   the   sun   from

_____

6. used   were   in   Scotland   umbrellas   in   1800's   the

_____

7. use   I   the   rain   umbrella   my   in

_____

D. Read each group of sentences. Find the sentence that does not belong and cross it out.

1. My mom bought me an umbrella. It was a present for my seventh birthday. It is red, blue, and yellow. It looks really neat. My mom made me a huge birthday cake.

2. I have a new umbrella. It is colourful. It was cloudy yesterday. I can use it in the rain and also in the sun.

3. My neighbour, Jenny, has an umbrella hat. It is an umbrella but it is also a hat. She wears it on her head. We often play together after school. She looks cute in her umbrella hat.

E. Draw a picture of a present that you received. Write three sentences about it.

13 Sam the Firefighter

Sam is a firefighter. He works at a station near my house. Sam and his friends fight fires, but they also do a lot of other work.

At the fire station, Sam works hard to make sure that all the equipment is clean and working well. There is a lot of equipment used by firefighters, like hoses and axes.

When Sam is on duty, he stays at the fire station for many hours at a time, sometimes overnight.

A. **Find these words in the passage above. Some letters have been given to you.**

1. f __ r __ f __ g __ t __ r

2. __ o __ k __

3. s __ a __ i __ n

4. e q __ i __ m __ n __

5. f __ i __ n __ s

6. d __ t __

7. h __ u __ s

8. h __ s __ s

9. h __ u __ e

10. c __ e __ n

11. s __ m __ t __ m __ s

12. o __ e __ n __ g __ t

B. **In each of the following passages, there is a sentence that does not belong. Find the sentence that does not belong and draw a line through it.**

1. There were lots of bluejays in the garden. They were eating seeds and sitting on tree branches. We had lunch there.

2. Sunflowers can grow almost as tall as a one-storey house. The apple is tasty. Even the sunflower seeds are pretty big.

3. William has a new red bike. He can ride it without training wheels. His sister has a toothache.

4. Jane liked the flowers. She went to school. She picked some flowers for her dad.

5. Vincent ran all the way to the park. He played on the monkey bars. William went shopping with his mom.

6. There are seven days in every week. Sunday is the first day of the week. I enjoyed the show. Saturday is the last day.

7. Our car was dirty. We went to the carwash yesterday. There are little flies in the bushes. Now the car is clean and shiny.

13

C. Read each sentence. Cross out ✗ the incorrect word.

*Words that sound the same but have different meanings are called **homonyms**.*

1. We (ate   eight) the corn.

2. The (bare   bear) lives in the woods.

3. Mary walked (buy   by) the car.

4. It takes 100 (cents   sense) to make $1.

5. The doctor checks my (wait   weight).

6. The girls took (sum   some) nuts.

7. Can you (hear   here) the music?

8. She (knew   new) the answer.

9. Judy picked the (flower   flour).

10. Will she (cell   sell) the candy to me?

11. I got stung by a (be   bee)!

12. The police (caught   court) the thieves.

D. These pictures tell about firefighters. Write a sentence about what is happening in each picture. You may use the words in the Word Bank to help you.

WORD BANK

firefighters	fight	fire truck
fire	pole	slide	hose

1. _____
_____
_____

2. _____
_____
_____

3. _____
_____
_____

4. _____
_____
_____

The cactus plant grows in the desert where it is hot in the day and cold at night. There is very little rainfall in the desert. When it does rain, the shallow roots soak up rainwater quickly. The stem of the cactus plant is fat and thick. It can expand to hold the water. This means that the plant still has water even when it does not rain for a long period of time.

Rebus Stories

Rebus means using pictures to take the place of words.

Example: sun ☀

A. Choose two sentences in the story and write them in rebus form.

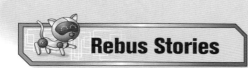

The 🌵 plant grows in the ～～ where it is very hot in the ☀ and cold at ☁.

1. _____

_____

2. _____

_____

B. Each of the sentences below has a misspelled word. Circle the misspelled word and write the correct spelling in the box.

1. The cactus plant grows in the dessert.

2. It also has shellow roots.

3. The cactas plant has a thick stem.

4. There is no rain for a long peried of time.

5. The stem expends to hold water.

6. The water gets stord in the stem.

7. The stem is fat and think.

8. There is little ranefall.

14

C. Each of these sentences has a word that does not make sense. Find a word that fits and write it above the one that doesn't.

Example: In the desert, it is ~~cold~~ **hot** in the day.

1. In the desert, it is hot at night.

2. There is very much rainfall.

3. In the desert, it does not rain for a short period of time.

4. The cactus roots soak up rainwater slowly.

5. The cactus stem is thin.

6. The cactus stem shrinks to hold water.

7. The roots of the cactus are thick.

D. Finish the sentences. You may use your own words.

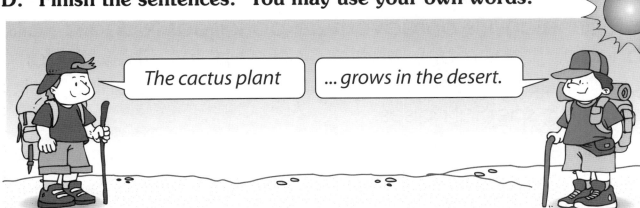

The cactus plant   ...grows in the desert.

1. A desert is _____ .

2. A cactus plant has _____ .

3. There is little _____ .

4. The cactus roots _____ .

5. The cactus stem _____ .

6. Water is stored _____ .

7. The days in the desert _____ .

8. The nights in the desert _____ .

15 Marineland

Marineland is an adventure park near Niagara Falls, Canada. It has many whales and dolphins. They perform tricks like eating food from your hand. The dolphins "talk" by making special noises.

Marineland is such a great place to spend a day. Besides the sea animals at Marineland, there are also lots of rides. The roller-coaster ride is the most exciting. There are also games to play and souvenirs to buy. You can buy lots of different kinds of foods too.

Marineland is so much fun!

A. Unscramble the sentences.

| Marineland | Canada | Niagara Falls | , | in | is | . |

1. _____

| There | animals | sea | are | there | . |

2. _____

| fun | so | There | in | Marineland | much | is | . |

3. _____

| rides | exciting | Roller-coaster | are | very | . |

4. _____

B. Complete the crossword puzzle.

Across

A A clever sea animal with a long nose

B Do

C An exciting ride

D An exciting place to visit

E Clever acts

Down

1 A huge sea animal

2 Things to buy

3 Opposite of "same"

4 A body of water like an ocean

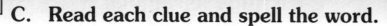

Marineland Scavenger Hunt →

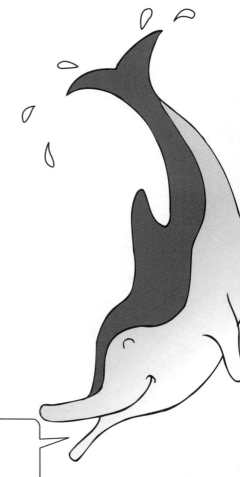

C. Read each clue and spell the word.

1 I come out at night and provide light.

⬤ __ __ __ __

2 I'm red and round, and I'm a fruit.

⬤ __ __ __ __ __

3 I'm the colour of an apple.

⬤ __ __ __

4 I'm a letter that sounds the same as "eye".

⬤ __

5 Birds live in me.

__ __ __ __

6 I'm the opposite of "difficult".

⬤ __ __ __ __

7 I'm a red bug with black spots.

__ __ __ __ __ __ __

8 I'm a little insect. I can't fly.

⬤ __ __ __

9 I'm the opposite of "day".

⬤ __ __ __ __

10 I'm a pet. I bark when I'm mad.

⬤ __ __ __

Now, write the circled letters in order.

__ __ __ __ __ __ __ __ __ __

D. The following pictures are about Marineland. Write a sentence about each.

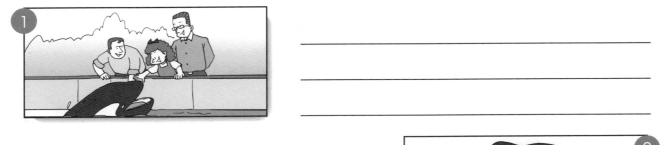

1 _____

_____

_____

2

_____

_____

3

_____

_____

_____

Challenge

Draw a picture of yourself doing fun things at Marineland and write a sentence to describe it.

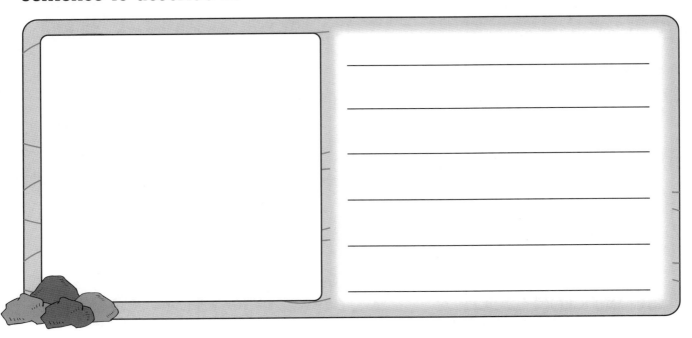

A. <u>Underline</u> the noun in each of the following phrases.

1 the cute doll

2 four new books

3 a new bike

4 a little cat

5 a spotted dog

6 six melting popsicles

7 the soft pillow

8 the brick house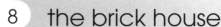

9 a funny clown

10 the green plant

11 a tidy bed

12 my first car

13 an empty glass

14 the bright light

15 a tall tree

16 his baseball cap

17 a pretty girl

18 a brave firefighter

19 a crowded street

20 a wooden box

21 a sunny day

22 a big breakfast

23 a winding road

24 a huge whale

B. Read the clues. Complete the crossword puzzle with the words that mean the opposite.

Across

A. small
B. full
C. hard
D. short
E. thin

Down

1. hate
2. no
3. slow
4. heavy
5. bright

C. Unscramble the sentences and write them on the lines.

Remember to begin each sentence with a capital letter and end it with a period.

1. favourite   are   my   candies   jujubes

   _____

2. is   Judy   good   friend   my   sister's

   _____

3. good   summer   ice cream   in   is   so

   _____

4. people   Toronto   visit   many   Zoo

   _____

5. swimming   I   go   like   to

   _____

6. read   of   we   lot   books   a

   _____

7. work   many   for   hours   firefighters

   _____

8. dolphins   sea   clever   animals   are

   _____

D. Read each of the following sentences. Circle the word in ( ) that means the same as the one in the shaded box.

1. The big dog jumped up on me.

   (large   tall)

2. There was a tiny kitten at the pet store.

   (tidy   small)

3. Mom walked very fast towards me.

   (quickly   carefully)

4. We have been to Marineland once .

   (one time   every time)

5. The clever boy answered all the questions.

   (smart   cute)

6. Look at my beautiful dress.

   (new   pretty)

7. My dad has a lot of work to do.

   (much   more)

8. Our neighbour is a nice old lady.

   (kind   rich)

E. Write a rhyming word for each of the following words.

1 rest

2 cup

3 sick

4 read

5 few

6 say

7 treat

8 real

9 four

10 rain

11 tale

12 burn

13 ate

14 land

15 stop

16 ever

17 care

18 neat

19 fill

20 paid

21 bug

22 give

23 pull

24 told

F. Each of the following sentences has a misspelled word. Circle the misspelled word and write the correct spelling in the box.

1. The trane arrives late.

2. Many peeple like to eat ice cream.

3. Jo and her fiends are playing in the park.

4. The bluejays are eating seads in the garden.

5. There are many advanture parks in Canada.

6. The plum is a juicy friut.

7. The children are petting the whale.

8. We had a picnic lunch on the glass.

9. Penquins are cute animals.

10. We play soccer in the big feeld.

1.	2.
3.	4.
5.	6.
7.	8.
9.	10.

1

Join each frog to a lily pad to form a word.

1. cl
2. gl
3. bla
4. sl
5. pl
6. fl

us
ue
ck
ag
ock
ed

2 Percy the Piglet wants to save his pocket money into a piggy bank. Colour the coins with "money" words to make a path to the piggy bank.

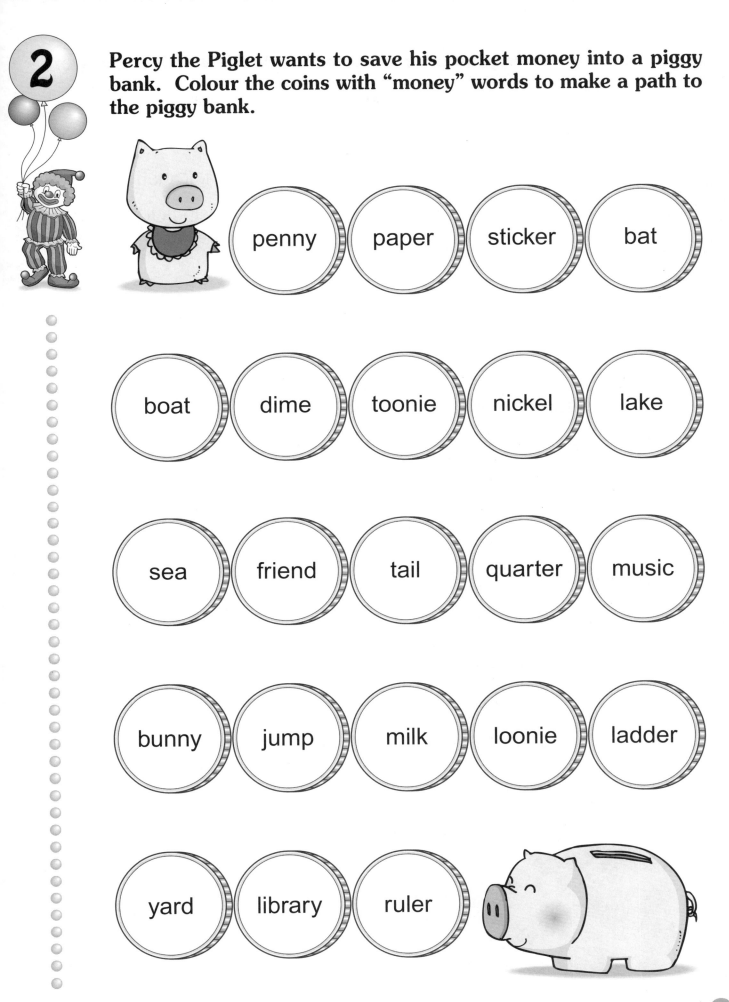

penny	paper	sticker	bat
boat	dime	toonie	nickel	lake
sea	friend	tail	quarter	music
bunny	jump	milk	loonie	ladder
yard	library	ruler

3

Nellie is having fun on the beach. Circle the words in the word search.

sunglasses   sand   umbrella
swimsuit   pail   sandcastle
lifebelt   seagull   spade
hat   towel   shell   sun

s	b	l	i	f	e	b	e	l	t
u	a	q	c	k	v	s	o	p	o
n	m	n	s	g	d	u	e	a	w
g	p	b	d	o	j	n	w	i	e
l	m	h	r	c	s	h	e	l	l
a	k	c	t	e	a	w	a	z	s
s	a	n	d	o	l	s	j	t	p
s	e	a	g	u	l	l	t	y	a
e	x	r	l	e	n	v	a	l	d
s	w	i	m	s	u	i	t	e	e

Circle the word that does not belong in each balloon.

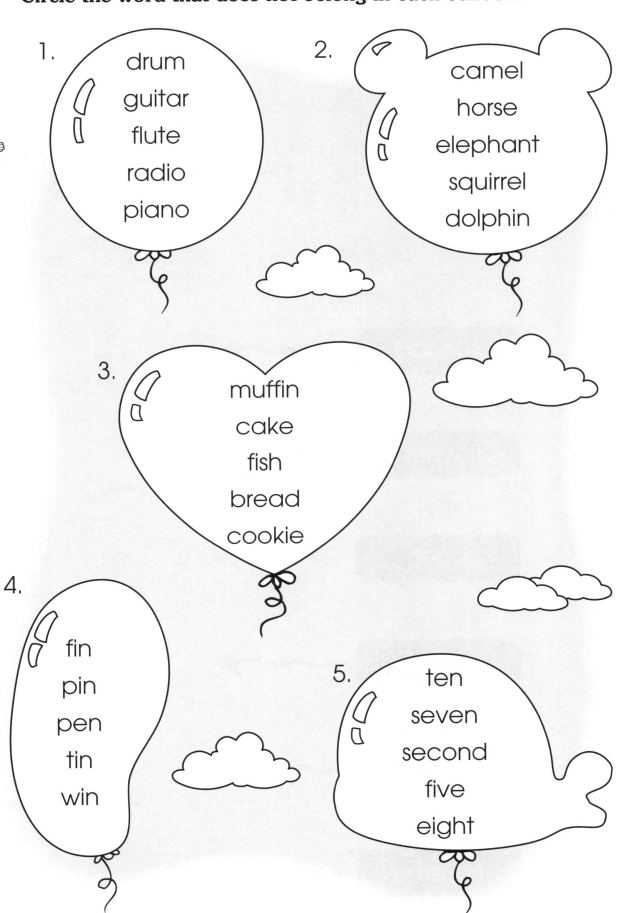

1.
drum
guitar
flute
radio
piano

2.
camel
horse
elephant
squirrel
dolphin

3.
muffin
cake
fish
bread
cookie

4.
fin
pin
pen
tin
win

5.
ten
seven
second
five
eight

5 Find one word hidden in each of the words. Write it in the .

chair

car

1. **second**

2. **flavour**

3. **paper**

4. **baked**

5. **special**

6. **house**

6 Count and colour the fish Uncle Fred has caught by following the letters in the words "A great catch". Write the number on the pail.

7 Read the clues and complete the crossword puzzle.

Across

1 This pet likes to run on a turning wheel.

4 A canary is one.

6 This pet may be named Porky.

7 If your pet rabbit was named King Rabbitoh, what would its initials be?

9 Another name for a rabbit

12 Birds need these to fly to their perch.

13 A bird's claws are its ____ .

Down

1 What pet cats like to drink

2 A pet frog or a pet snake may lay these.

3 We keep these in a bowl or tank.

5 This pet has been called "Man's Best Friend".

8 Bugs Bunny is one.

10 Rabbits like to twitch their ____ .

11 Pet birds are kept in a ____ .

8

Look at the cute baby animals. Write what they are.

piglet   cub   puppy

duckling   fawn   calf

1.   I'm a _____ .

2.   I'm a _____ .

3.   I'm a _____ .

4.   I'm a _____ .

5.   I'm a _____ .

6.   I'm a _____ .

9

Put the puzzle pieces in the correct places. Write the letters on the blank pieces. What does each picture show?

10 Help Liz the Lizard find her way up the wall by colouring the two-syllable words.

reporter	block	kitten	easier
old	today	furry
together	under	toast	hen
through	behind	winter
sail	cheap	ring	pocket
family	sister	balloon

11 Match the clouds with words that rhyme. Colour each pair the same colour.

dot

ink

talk

boat

cake

spot

bake

pink

swim

dim

float

walk

12 Sandra and her classmates are visiting the farm. Circle the animals in the word search.

duck	sheep	horse	goat
pig	goose	turkey	rabbit
cow	chicken	pigeon	dog

c	m	g	o	s	p	r	a	c	x	a	p
g	h	o	r	s	e	a	f	o	t	c	i
k	d	t	a	h	o	d	u	p	e	l	e
n	y	x	b	k	c	o	w	i	t	o	s
s	a	u	b	c	t	g	o	g	a	q	h
o	e	d	i	g	o	o	s	e	b	a	e
d	t	u	t	p	a	r	a	o	b	t	e
v	m	c	h	i	c	k	e	n	i	b	p
g	c	k	d	g	d	s	m	h	f	w	r
o	r	c	n	v	p	z	e	z	q	x	n
a	j	u	o	a	x	g	b	y	u	d	w
t	u	r	k	e	y	c	s	b	v	t	k

13 Help Monica open the treasure chest by entering the code. Follow the letters in the words "treasure hunt" to get the code.

t r e s u n ☽ ◇ ☽

e r a e w t △ ♡ △

a u s u n t ☆ ○ ☆

b r e h n t Ⓢ ♡ Ⓢ

Enter Code

14 Help the zookeeper write the names of the animals.

1.

2.

3.

4.

5.

6.

15

Read the clues and complete the crossword puzzle.

Across

1. A worker bee has this many stings.

3. These are also stinging insects.

6. This insect can be annoying and it may carry diseases.

8. These jumping insects make a shrill chirping sound.

9. An insect with hard feelers (some are tiny but others are quite large)

11. These insects can spoil your picnic!

Down

2. Where wasps and other insects lay their eggs

4. These tiny insects can carry heavy loads.

5. A queen bee does this to other queens.

6. This insect of the night is attracted by light.

7. Some people think most insects are ____ .

8. People walk but creepy crawlies ____ .

9. Its home is a hive.

10. An insect hatches from this.

16 Help Mother Hen find her eggs by colouring the eggs that rhyme with "hen".

mend

ban

pan

tent

ten

fen

lent

Ben

send

glen

mean

lend

yen

fan

den

men

pen

17

Little Carol wants to make an animal-sticker album. Help her colour the stickers with "animal" words.

walrus   penguin   tiger   Sticker Album

cheetah   sock   belt   sweater

skunk   fox   beaver   jumper

boots   tie   ostrich   skirt

vest   wolf   rabbit   blouse

whale   bow   coat

18

Find ten "colour" words in the word search.
Colour the picture with all the ten colours.

c	p	k	g	s	f	r	e	l	a	p	h
f	i	q	x	m	o	w	h	i	t	e	n
h	n	b	p	c	u	b	l	y	v	k	i
d	k	a	o	w	g	r	e	e	n	o	t
b	g	t	r	n	c	o	j	l	w	x	f
l	m	e	a	y	m	w	b	l	u	e	r
a	i	p	n	d	g	n	h	o	a	s	d
c	n	u	g	r	q	i	t	w	l	z	j
k	s	r	e	d	k	z	c	o	q	b	v
o	j	a	v	e	p	u	r	p	l	e	m

19

Look at the code and the pictures. Write what Lilian says.

1	2	3	4	5	6	7	8	9	10	11	12	13
A	B	C	D	E	F	G	H	I	J	K	L	M

14	15	16	17	18	19	20	21	22	23	24	25	26
N	O	P	Q	R	S	T	U	V	W	X	Y	Z

13, 25   14, 1, 21, 7, 8, 20, 25

8, 9, 4, 5, 19   8, 9, 19   6, 1, 22, 15, 21, 18, 9, 20, 5

 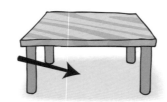 13, 25

_____

_____

_____

_____

20 Read the clues and complete the crossword puzzle.

Across

1 This very large fruit is green on the outside and red and watery on the inside; it has black seeds.

4 A juicy yellow or green fruit shaped a bit like a heart

6 Fruits are nice to ____ .

7 Before eating an orange, you must ____ it.

9 A yellow fruit with a stone inside

10 Strawberries are this colour.

Down

2 This fruit can be green, red, or yellow; it has a core.

3 The name of this fruit is the same as its colour.

5 You should only eat fruits if they are ____ ; otherwise you might get a stomach ache.

7 This soft pink fruit is fleshy and has a large stone inside.

8 Taste of a lemon

1 The Bumblebee

A. 1. It is an insect.
   2. It is yellow and black.
   3. The queen bee is the leader.
   4. She lays eggs after a winter in hibernation.
B. 1. leaf   2. cap
   3. bat   4. jug
   5. yarn   6. wagon
   7. goat   8. rabbit
   9. duck   10. top
   11. fan   12. queen
   13. sun   14. hat
C. 1. Polar bears live in the Arctic. They are big and white. <u>Big paws.</u> They have small eyes and ears. <u>Jump from ice floe to ice floe.</u>
   2. Polar bears have other names. <u>Sometimes called white bears, sea bears, or ice bears.</u> <u>Swim very well.</u>
   3. Polar bears move fast and travel far. <u>Eat seals and fish.</u> The male is usually larger than the female. <u>Hairy feet.</u>
   4. Baby bears or cubs are born in winter. <u>Weigh 2 pounds when born.</u> <u>Remain with mothers from 10 months to 2 years.</u>
D. 1. A square is a shape with four equal sides.
   2. A triangle is a shape with three sides.
   3. A circle is a single line.
   4. A rectangle is a shape with opposite sides that are equal.

2 The Museum Trip

A. 1. B   2. B
   3. B   4. C
B. 1. bus   2. box
   3. nest   4. dime
   5. tulip   6. mask
   7. bar   8. pot
   9. pen   10. bone
   11. can   12. ball
   13. sock   14. saw
   15. kite   16. rake
C. 1. Apples   2. The CN Tower
   3. The Earth   4. A computer
   5. Skating   6. The time
   7. (Individual drawing and answer)
D. 1. Hockey   2. Baseball
   3. Hockey ; Baseball   4. Hockey
   5. Baseball   6. Hockey
   7. Baseball   8. Hockey ; Baseball

3 The Eurotunnel

A. 1. England and France
   2. In 1993
   3. Napoleon
   4. Two are for trains to carry people and one is for emergency and service.
B. 1. lamp   2. web
   3. mop   4. jug
   5. pot   6. bag
   7. desk   8. bell
   9. net   10. can
   11. lips   12. fan
   13. tent   14. rock
   15. six   16. nut
C. (Individual writing)
D. 1. cup ; bowl ; glass
   2. blackboard ; desk ; eraser
   3. tires ; horn ; key
   4. swing ; seesaw ; slide
   5. pear ; grapes ; apple

4 Snakes

A. 1. reptiles   2. long
   3. cold   4. eggs
   5. laid   6. hibernation
   7. skins   8. move
   9. place
B. 1. bike   2. hive
   3. pole   4. cone
   5. cake   6. tube
   7. kite   8. ruler
   9. gate   10. tulip
C. (Order may vary.)
   1. At the zoo, we visit the animals.
   2. The monkey likes to hang by its tail.
   3. The African elephant is the largest living land animal.
   4. The zebra is black and white.
   5. The male lion has a mane on its neck.
   6. The tiger is orange and black.
   7. The zookeeper helps clean the cages.
D. 1. recipe
   2. box
   3. ingredients
   4. cupboard
   5. refrigerator
   6. pot ; stove ; melted
   7. square

5 What Happens Next?

A. (Individual writing)

B.
1.	snail	2.	day
3.	nail	4.	jay
5.	tray	6.	paint
7.	tail	8.	pay
9.	say	10.	play

C.
1. We start school in autumn.
2. My school is close to home.
3. I walk to and from school every day.
4. Sometimes, I go home for lunch.
5. There are lots of sports at my school.
6. We play hockey, soccer, and volleyball. / We play soccer, hockey, and volleyball.
7. I like to play floor games.

D.

q	w	f	s	w	h	o	f	x	f	h	k	t
h	b	k	n	e	b	k	r	b	h	l	g	r
r	o	x	a	l	m	n	o	k	l	w	z	a
p	k	f	i	q	a	g	z	l	z	s	n	i
q	g	c	l	a	y	o	c	z	n	a	i	l
r	o	e	q	c	d	k	d	r	f	y	j	h
b	h	q	t	e	l	f	e	s	w	e	h	f
q	x	o	r	v	b	p	r	a	y	r	l	n
z	d	r	a	f	w	f	w	d	n	p	q	l
p	l	a	y	w	o	x	o	r	s	t	j	s
s	t	x	x	h	e	d	x	h	x	a	x	h
g	d	h	b	o	l	k	b	c	h	r	i	m
r	a	o	f	r	b	s	l	e	t	s	g	l
h	y	m	l	x	m	l	b	x	n	a	y	b

6 Days of the Week

A. (Suggested answers)
2. On Monday, Ben will go to the beach.
3. On Tuesday, he will go on the roller coaster.
4. On Wednesday, he will go to the library.
5. On Thursday, he will paint a picture.
6. On Friday, he will go to the children's playground.
7. (Individual drawing and writing)

B.
1.	bee	2.	jeans
3.	tea	4.	team
5.	bean	6.	meat
7.	weed	8.	week
9.	sea	10.	seed

C. (Individual colouring and writing)

D. **Months of the Year:**
January ; February ; March ; April ; May ; June ; July ; August ; September ; October ; November ; December

Days of the Week:
Sunday ; Monday ; Tuesday ; Wednesday ; Thursday ; Friday ; Saturday

7 The CN Tower

A.
1. The CN Tower is the tallest self-supporting tower in the world.
2. It is as high as five and a half football fields.
3. Its foundation is as deep as a five-storey building.
4. The CN Tower was built to improve the broadcasting of radio and television signals.
5. One of the world records at the CN Tower was a person hopping down its 1,967 steps on a pogo stick.

B.
1.	flowers	2.	clowns
3.	slide	4.	black
5.	glass	6.	sled
7.	flag	8.	blew
9.	plate	10.	glad
11.	clock	12.	play

C. (Individual writing)

D. (Suggested drawings)

1.

2.

3.

4.

5.

6.

8 Sir John A. Macdonald

A.
1. Sir John A. Macdonald
2. Glasgow, Scotland
3. Five
4. In 1867
5. The completion of the Pacific Railway

B. (Suggested answers)
prune ; prime ; crop
grip ; grape ; bring
cream ; fruit ; braid
grass ; drone ; prize

trap ; tree ; frog
drum ; dress ; truck
crab ; trail ; true
broom ; breed ; frame
green ; crime ; cross
free ; frail ; groom

C.   (Individual writing)

D.   1.   the first
     2.   the eighth
     3.   the second
     4.   the sixth
     5.   the fifth
     6.   the fourth
     7.   the seventh
     8.   the ninth
     9.   the third
     10. the tenth

9   Dance Lessons

A.   1.   ballet   2.   slippers
     3.   day   4.   ten
     5.   many   6.   good
     7.   dance   8.   costumes
     9.   fun   10. jive

B.   1.   smells   2.   space
     3.   stairs   4.   stove
     5.   skunk   6.   snake
     7.   snack   8.   swim
     9.   skip   10. small
     11. swat   12. snip
     13. snap   14. spoon

C.   1.   Fetch the bone, Punkie.
     2.   Punkie, go and get the newspaper.
     3.   Find the shoe, Punkie.
     4.   Take the leash in your mouth.
     5.   Find the toy.
     6.   Don't chase the car.

D.   1.   penny   2.   toonie
     3.   dime   4.   quarter
     5.   loonie   6.   nickel

Progress Test 1

A.   1.   road ; toad ; load
     2.   like ; bike ; hike ; Pike
     3.   game ; came ; tame ; name
     4.   bake ; take ; cake ; lake ; rake
     5.   day ; Jay ; ray ; say ; way ; May

B.   1.   vase   2.   acorn
     3.   jug   4.   pin
     5.   nest   6.   gate
     7.   mop   8.   leaf

     9.   fan   10. yarn
     11. hat   12. sock
     13. web   14. six
     15. cap

C.   1.   tube   2.   cake
     3.   log   4.   bone
     5.   pole   6.   hive
     7.   tent   8.   fish
     9.   cube   10. rake
     11. five   12. hand

D.

E.   1.   . ; T   2.   ? ; A
     3.   . ; I   4.   ? ; A
     5.   ! ; S   6.   . ; I
     7.   ! ; S

F.   1.   (The car) drove down the highway.
     2.   (The bird) laid the eggs in the nest.
     3.   (Mom) bakes great cakes at home.
     4.   (Tom) walks to school every day.
     5.   (She) likes to take the dog for a walk.

G.   1.   B   2.   G
     3.   C   4.   D
     5.   E   6.   F
     7.   A

H.   (Individual answers)

10   The Treasure Chest

A.   (Suggested answers)
     1.   Rob heard about a sunken ship in Sharaz.
     2.   They decided to search for the sunken treasure.

B.   1.   Ch ; ch ; ch ; ch   2.   Sh ; sh ; sh
     3.   Th ; th ; th ; th ; th
     4.   wh ; wh ; wh ; wh ; wh ; wh ; wh

C.   1.   whiskers   2.   thick
     3.   ship   4.   chest
     5.   peach   6.   moth

D.   1.   dogs   2.   mats
     3.   acorns   4.   desks

5. ships
6. tables
7. bears
8. girls
9. rulers
10. lakes
11. boats
12. roads
13. toys
14. trees
15. flowers
16. plants
17. rugs
18. flags
19. boys
20. masks

E.
1. horse
2. cow
3. rabbit
4. dog
5. kangaroo
6. pig
7. chicken
8. goose
9. cat
10. deer

11 A Visit to the Farm

A.
1. There are different kinds of farms.
2. They visited a dairy farm.
3. He used big machines.

B.   Arnie's <u>farm</u> is <u>far</u> from the <u>market</u>. Every day, Arnie <u>works</u> very <u>hard</u>. He <u>turns</u> the soil, which is sometimes called <u>dirt</u>. When there are lots of <u>worms</u> in the soil, it is healthy. There are also lots of animals on the <u>farm</u>. Some are <u>horses</u> and others are pigs, from which Arnie gets <u>pork</u> to sell at the market.

C.
1. Mark
2. Ottawa
3. Venus
4. Mrs. Smith
5. Sun
6. Punkie
7. Portland Drive
8. Mars
9. Canada Day
10. Sunday
11. The Gap
12. Charlotte's Web
13. Deer Lake
14. May

D.
1. English
2. Spanish
3. France
4. Hungarian
5. Romanian
6. Italian
7. Greek

E.
1. ITALIAN
2. SPANISH
3. HUNGARIAN

12 Out on the Road

A.
1. A
2. F
3. E
4. D
5. C
6. B

B.
clown: town ; brown ; flowers ; crown
house: hound ; blouse ; couch ; mouse ; sound
snowman: grow ; blow ; row ; glow ; rainbow ; low

C.
six street lights ; four cars
ten flowers ; two boys
five bicycles ; seven trees
nine parking meters ; three trucks

D.
1. G
2. F
3. B
4. H
5. A
6. D
7. C
8. E

13 The Coin Collection

A.
1. David has a coin collection.
2. He has over three hundred coins.
3. His first coins were from Italy.
4. Many people have given him coins for gifts.
5. He has coins from all over the world.
6. David's favourite coin is one from Sri Lanka.
7. His favourite coin is large and heavy.
8. A Chinese coin has a hole in the centre.

B.
1. loyal
2. coin
3. boy
4. joy
5. point
6. soy
7. annoy
8. boil
9. toy
10. Oil

C. (Individual writing)

D.
1. crying
2. breezy
3. tired
4. little
5. damp
6. big
7. hard
8. dirty

14 Making Blueberry Muffins

A.
1. muffins
2. wet
3. blueberries
4. egg
5. 400°F

B.
1. cook
2. book
3. look
4. cookbook
5. fool
6. pool
7. cool
8. drool

C.
1. is
2. are
3. is
4. is
5. are
6. are
7. are
8. am
9. is
10. is

D.
1. cold
2. short
3. thin
4. wet
5. sad
6. healthy
7. white
8. brave
9. answer

F.
1. S
2. H
3. A
4. A
5. S
6. A
7. A
8. A
9. H

15 A Balloon Ride

A.
1. F ; It was a sunny morning.
2. T
3. F ; The balloon was in the park.
4. F ; The balloon lifted off slowly.

B.
1. half
2. talk
3. stalk
4. walk
5. calf
6. palm

C.
1. lamb
2. crumb
3. thumb
4. limb

D.
1. are
2. has
3. build
4. live
5. consists
6. breed

E.
1. hot ; cold
2. early ; late
3. best ; worst ; calm ; windy
4. opened ; closed ; up ; down

F. (Individual writing)

16 Autumn

A.
1. season
2. summer
3. fall
4. beautiful
5. because
6. colour
7. ground
8. carpet
9. hike
10. animals
11. woods
12. fawns
13. woods

B.
1. Autumn follows summer.
2. They change colour and fall to the ground.
3. We find them in woods near cities.
4. Another name for autumn is fall.
5. Winter comes after autumn.

C.
1. fawn
2. jaw
3. straw
4. auto
5. saw
6. autumn
7. saucer
8. yawn

D.
1. The tired boys rested under the shady tree.
2. He put a big book into a small bag.
3. The friendly nurse is helping the sick girl.
4. The old man is talking to the young child.
5. She picked a red apple from the tall tree.
6. The black puppy is playing with a red ball.

E. (Individual writing)

17 All about Plants

A.
1. They start as a seed.
2. They usually plant them in the garden or the yard.
3. They cover it with soil.
4. It takes a few weeks for shoots to sprout.

B.

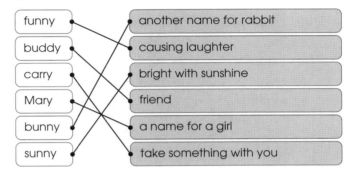

funny — causing laughter
buddy — friend
carry — take something with you
Mary — a name for a girl
bunny — another name for rabbit
sunny — bright with sunshine

C.
1. Why
2. try
3. fly
4. shy
5. my

D.
```
        3       4
   A P L A N T E D
     L     N
   1 A     S     5
   T Y   B W A N T E D
   R E     E     E
   E   2   R     E
   A   S   E     D
 C T R A I N E D  D E N D E D
   E   I           D
   D   L
 E L E A R N E D
     D
```

E.
1. December
2. September
3. February
4. October
5. January
6. June
7. August
8. November
9. March
10. May
11. July

18   Penguins

A.
1. Antarctica ; Africa ; Australia
2. Blue Fairy
3. 40 cm
4. Emperor
5. fish ; squid ; shrimp
6. female penguin ; male

B.
SOFT c: city ; civil ; cent
HARD c: create ; cake ; clown ; cook
SOFT g: giant ; gym ; gem ; giraffe
HARD g: gate ; grow ; goose ; girl

C.
1. write — wrote
2. drink — drank
3. ring — rang
4. think — thought
5. drive — drove
6. leave — left

D.
1. eat
2. go
3. run
4. swim
5. lose
6. make

E.

z	b	y	d	i	s	k	e	t	t	e	s
o	u	n	o	q	c	k	b	s	j	x	c
j	p	r	i	n	t	e	r	a	l	b	o
k	d	b	i	a	b	y	o	f	e	u	m
o	e	a	u	e	u	b	h	c	j	i	p
r	u	f	c	r	m	o	d	e	m	b	u
i	c	t	d	s	c	a	o	n	e	r	t
m	o	n	i	t	o	r	d	k	e	l	e
j	v	s	i	w	o	d	h	g	s	k	r

Progress Test 2

A.
1. oceans
2. small
3. plates
4. chew
5. whole
6. length
7. weigh
8. smell
9. pitches
10. breathing

B. David and his friend, Judy, are going to visit the Hockey Hall of Fame in downtown Toronto, Canada. It is in a large building not far from Union Station, where the friends are taking the subway from Mississauga to Toronto.

There are so many exciting exhibits at the Hockey Hall of Fame. There are pieces of equipment worn by famous hockey players, like Wayne Gretzky. The Stanley Cup, which is awarded to the top hockey team each year, is sometimes on display there.

The children want to see the first mask that was worn by Jacques Plante and some of the old hockey uniforms from years gone by. Maybe, if they're lucky, they might see a visiting hockey player.

The last thing David and Judy go to see is all the statistics of players who broke many records over the years. Players like Gordie Howe, Jean Beliveau, and Wayne Gretzky changed the game of hockey forever.

C. Canada ; largest ; North America ; ten ; three ; Nunavut ; four ; three ; Maritime ; three

D.
1. is
2. like
3. plays
4. studied
5. takes
6. have
7. laughs
8. is
9. fixed
10. am

E. (Individual writing)

F.
1. sale
2. sea
3. pear
4. mail
5. blue
6. vane

G.
1. large
2. cry
3. tiny
4. run
5. hop
6. sad

H.
1. bright
2. dry
3. clean
4. close
5. happy
6. heavy

I.
1. e
2. i
3. e
4. i
5. i
6. i
7. e
8. e
9. i
10. e
11. e
12. e
13. e
14. i
15. e

1 Nouns

A. Common Noun: lollipop ; car ; lake ; rainbow
   Proper Noun: Beatrice ; April ; Christmas ; Thursday

B. 1. sweets
   2. chicks
   3. apple
   4. rat
   5. kids
   6. parrot

C.

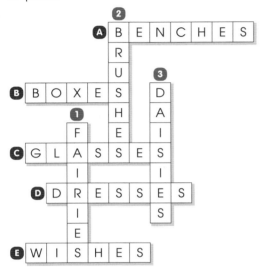

D. 1. kitten
   2. water ; cups
   3. squirrels
   4. plastic
   5. sand ; pots
   6. dollars
   7. hay ; barn
   8. furniture

2 Pronouns

A. 1. We   2. I
   3. I   4. He
   5. We ; It   6. I ; They
   7. She

B. 1. We   2. He
   3. It   4. They
   5. She   6. It

C. 1. They take us to the zoo.
   2. We go to see the zebras first.
   3. He takes pictures of the zebras.
   4. It looks at us.

D. us: Lily and me ; our class
   him: the policeman ; Kevin the Clown
   her: my sister ; the little girl

it: Kate's hamster ; his tall hat
them: the cows ; Mr. and Mrs. Hall

E. 1. it
   2. me ; you
   3. them
   4. him
   5. us
   6. her

F. (Individual writing)

3 Articles

A. a: unit ; river ; house ; violin
   an: album ; error ; idea ; umbrella
   the: South Pole ; RCMP ; CN Tower ; St. Lawrence River

B.

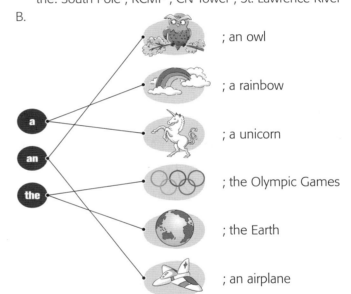

; an owl
; a rainbow
; a unicorn
; the Olympic Games
; the Earth
; an airplane

C. 1. the
   2. an ; a
   3. the ; the
   4. The
   5. the ; the ; a
   6. the ; an
   7. A
   8. an
   9. the

D. 1. a ; huge
   2. a ; European
   3. an ; oval
   4. an ; unkind
   5. the ; Canadian
   6. an ; icy
   7. the ; Prime
   8. the ; Great

4 Present Tense Verbs

A. 1. sings ; singing
2. starts ; starting
3. listen ; listens
4. gathers ; gathering
5. walk ; walks
6. laugh ; laughing
7. breaks ; breaking
8. visit ; visiting

B. 1. shines   2. walking
3. chat   4. live
5. looking

C. 1. eat   2. gets
3. stay   4. blowing
5. ✔

D. 1. are   2. is
3. am   4. is
5. am   6. are
7. are

E. (Individual writing)

5 Past Tense Verbs

A. 1. closed   2. scored
3. lifted   4. brushed
5. erased   6. reached
7. collected   8. disliked

B. 1. carried   2. learned
3. skipped   4. hurried
5. stopped   6. grabbed
7. tried   8. preferred

C.

D. 1. ✘ ; It was raining when he walked his dog.
2. ✔
3. ✘ ; The kids were singing when the teacher came in.
4. ✘ ; Hilary and I were at the show last night.

6 Adjectives

A. 1. tall
2. a naughty dog
3. three marbles
4. an angry boy
5. a scary house
6. a freezing night

B. 1. lazy
2. Green
3. juicy
4. seven
5. round
6. hot
7. new ; yellow
8. black ; white ; fresh
9. puzzled

C. (Individual answers for the new adjectives)
(Circle these adjectives.)
1. pretty
2. interesting
3. six
4. red
5. hot
6. scary
7. scorching
8. great

D. (Individual colouring and writing)

Progress Test 1

A. (Circle these words.)
Colourland ; King Edwin ; Coby ; Coby ; Colourland
Coby
King Edwin ; Coby
Princess Lilian ; Prince Ned ; Coby

B. Countable Singular: kingdom ; place ; elf ; chance
Countable Plural: tricks ; colours ; hands
Uncountable: parchment ; luck
All these words are <u>common</u> nouns.

C. 1. she   2. I   3. We
4. they   5. It   6. You
7. He

D. 1. the   2. the   3. a
4. the   5. the   6. the

7. the   8. a   9. An

10. a   11. the   12. a

E. 1. wants
2. says
3. ask
4. explains ; is
5. is ; find
6. are
7. pacing ; biting
8. am

F. 1. The children found it hard to decide on what to look for first.
2. They were afraid that they might make the wrong guess.
3. They stayed right beyond the kingdom for the whole afternoon.
4. The colourless sun was setting and it was getting dark.
5. The first day of their quest slipped away quietly.

G. 1. three
2. round
3. happy
4. loud
5. blue
6. sure
7. colourless
8. small
9. sweet
10. very
11. boring

7   Prepositions

A. 1. in
2. behind
3. over
4. at ; near
5. on ; by
6. between
7. under ; beside

B. 1. on   2. beside
3. on   4. in
5. on   6. in
7. behind   8. from
9. on   10. around

C. 1. on   2. in
3. at   4. in
5. on   6. at
7. on

D. 1. on   2. ✔
3. at   4. ✔
5. at   6. ✔
7. on   8. in
9. at   10. on
11. ✔   12. on

8   Sentences

A. 1. ✔   2. ✗
3. ✗   4. ✔
5. ✔   6. ✗
7. ✔   8. ✗

B. 1. Mrs. Maddison
2. Brad's father
3. The children
4. Brad
5. Nina
6. The birthday cake
7. They
8. Andy
9. Brad's parents
10. The party

C. 1. can go cherry-picking in July
2. is a Christmas carol
3. is working on his Science project
4. are closed on New Year's Day
5. need a stick to play hockey
6. have pizza for lunch
7. is in front of the park
8. is wearing a pink skirt
9. is sick today
10. is feeding her babies
11. like eating worms

D. 1. C   2. E   3. A
4. D   5. B

E. (Individual writing)

9   Types of Sentences

A. 1. I   2. T   3. I
4. T   5. I   6. T

B. 1. It snows in winter.
2. They are sitting at the table.
3. This is made of glass.
4. The news in on at nine.

C. 1. Turn down the volume of the TV.
2. Don't shout at others.
3. Tell me the truth.
4. Write your name on the front page.

D. 1. ! ; E   2. ! ; E
    3. ? ; A   4. ! ; E
    5. ? ; A   6. ? ; A
    7. ! ; E   8. ? ; A
    9. ! ; E

E. 1. When is Mother's Day?
    2. What can we put in the salad?
    3. How old are you?
    4. Where is the dog?

F. (Individual writing)

10 Punctuation and Capitalization

A. 1. .   2. ?
    3. !   4. ?
    5. ✔   6. ✔

B. 1. ?   2. .
    3. ?   4. .
    5. .   6. .
    7. .   8. !
    9. .

C. 1. Beauty and the Beast
    2. Anne of Green Gables
    3. The Prince and the Pauper
    4. The Emperor's New Clothes
    5. Goldilocks and the Three Bears
    6. The Water Horse: Legend of the Deep

D. 1. I went trick-or-treating with my friends on Halloween night.
    2. It was a Friday.
    3. Jennifer dressed up as a witch.
    4. Ryan wanted a "Spiderman" costume.
    5. My neighbour, Mrs. Jevon, gave us lots of treats.
    6. Jennifer, Ryan, and I then enjoyed our treats together.

11 Forming Sentences

A. 1. The girl is pointing at the bird.
    2. The beaver is building a dam.
    3. The hamburger is on the plate.
    4. The lion is chasing the rat.

B. 1. The children are at a campsite.
    2. They are putting up a tent.
    3. They have a very big tent.
    4. They put their backpacks on the grass.
    5. Norman sees a raccoon.
    6. It is looking for food.
    7. There is a bear behind the tree.

C. (Put a line through these sentences.)
    1. The children are in the backyard.
    2. Jane is the youngest in her family.
    3. It is a sunny day.
    4. The fishermen's boat is big.
    5. Sunday is the first day of the week.

D. 1. 3 ; 4 ; 2 ; 1
    2. 4 ; 2 ; 1 ; 3

12 Forming Negative Sentences

A. 1. are not ; twins
    2. is not ; my neighbour
    3. am not ; a girl
    4. are not ; functioning well
    5. is not ; singing in the nest

B. 1. was not
    2. were not
    3. was not
    4. were not

C. 1. They were not singing when the bell rang.
    2. Sue was not at home when Jane called.

D. I: do not dance ; do not join ; do not drink
    Macy: does not swim ; does not dance ; does not join ; does not drink
    Ann and Roy: do not swim ; do not dance ; do not join ; do not drink

E. 1. Jamie does not like playing baseball.
    2. I do not go fishing with my dad.
    3. Mr. and Mrs. Moore do not want to live in the city.

F. 1. did not play
    2. did not go
    3. did not visit
    4. did not study

G. 1. Jason did not play video games yesterday.
    2. I did not come first in the race.

13 Synonyms, Antonyms, and Homonyms

A. 1. answer – solution
    2. clever – smart
    3. wrong – incorrect
    4. fix – repair
    5. make – build
    6. stop – halt
    7. change – alter
    8. funny – humorous

B. stay: depart ; go ; leave
    sad: glad ; happy ; jolly

slow: swift ; fast ; speedy

easy: difficult ; hard ; challenging

wrong: correct ; right ; proper

C. 1. oar ; or ; ore

2. tale ; tail

3. hare ; hair

4. blue ; blew

5. sow ; sew ; so

6. tow ; toe

7. sent ; scent ; cent

D.

D. 1. The children came to another tree.

2. There were many fruits in the tree.

3. Are they oranges or grapefruits?

4. Should we say "orange" or "yellow"?

5. We can eat one of them.

6. They found out that it was an orange tree.

7. They retrieved the colour orange.

E. 4 ; 1 ; 6 ; 2 ; 3 ; 5

F. 1. were not

2. was not difficult

3. were not

4. did not want

G. (Suggested answers)

1. long

2. red

3. returned

4. Everyone

5. cheered

6. appeared

7. happily

8. seem

9. be

10. next

11. great

12. air

Progress Test 2

A. 1. In

2. on

3. on

4. At

5. at

6. in

7. under

B. 1. F

2. C

3. B

4. E

5. H

6. G

7. D

8. A

C. 1. Can we do the same with the leaves?

2. No, we can't!

3. Leaves are not always green.

4. They change colours in fall and winter.

5. Don't you know it's summer now?

6. Lilian, touch the leaves and say the colour.

7. Ned, say the magic words.

8. Great, the colour green is back!

Types of Sentences

Telling: 3 ; 4

Imperative: 6 ; 7

Asking: 1 ; 5

Exclamatory: 2 ; 8

1 The Five Senses

A. smell – nose ; scent ; nostrils
  see   – lids ; eyes ; picture
  hear – ears ; loud ; sound
  taste – sweet ; tongue ; sour
  touch – fingers ; palm ; hard

B. 1. human   2. scent
  3. hearing   4. bones
  5. hand   6. hear
  7. taste   8. touch

C.
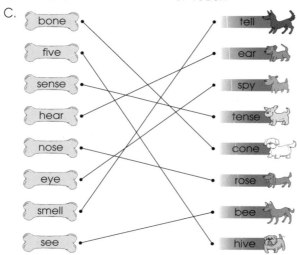

D. 1. hand   2. smell
  3. taste   4. bones
  5. touch   6. sense
  7. eyes   8. human
  9. sight   10. ears
  11. nose   12. hear

E.

k	y	d	m	s	c	u	s	i	g	h	t	b	z
x	w	t	u	g	k	m	h	e	o	d	f	h	i
b	d	o	f	j	e	c	o	k	h	q	t	s	u
p	w	n	r	v	a	f	t	o	u	c	h	w	o
d	k	g	k	u	r	i	w	y	m	b	p	v	l
a	z	u	h	l	s	q	b	g	a	o	o	m	h
s	e	e	c	p	x	u	h	a	n	d	t	f	e
y	i	t	f	v	j	a	o	l	u	y	d	x	a
g	p	s	m	e	l	l	w	q	c	j	m	i	r
k	m	o	r	y	o	y	b	i	g	b	v	l	c
t	a	s	t	e	r	t	o	z	r	o	n	r	q
h	c	u	w	s	j	v	n	o	s	e	h	m	k
w	i	p	s	e	n	s	e	b	l	f	i	v	e
n	l	b	c	r	b	f	s	h	x	p	d	t	i

2 Changing Seasons

A. spring   – warmer
         – buds
         – March
  summer – August
         – hot
         – June
  fall   – orange
         – yellow
         – brown
  winter   – snow
         – December
         – precipitation

B.

C. (Suggested answers)
  1. cud ; mud   2. dot ; got
  3. bow ; low   4. bee ; see
  5. down ; gown   6. heaves ; weaves

D. 1. four   2. fall
  3. grass   4. snow
  5. year   6. brown
  7. season   8. warmer
  9. trees

E. 1. The leaves are green.
  2. Leaves are in many colours.
  3. There are four seasons in every year.
  4. Spring begins in March and ends in June.
  5. Snow is a type of precipitation.
  6. Each season is about three months long.

3 The Butterfly

A. 1. egg 2. caterpillar
   3. pupa 4. butterfly
B. 1. female 2. pupa
   3. butterfly 4. nectar
   5. colourful
C. (Suggested answers)
   1. maid ; paid 2. bat ; cat
   3. dew ; new 4. corn ; horn
   5. pale ; sale 6. hot ; pot
D. 1. egg 2. leaf
   3. caterpillar 4. pupa
   5. butterfly 6. flowers
   7. fruits
E. (Individual writing)

4 Crispy Squares

A. 1. rice 2. bowl
   3. cups 4. crispy
   5. pour 6. stove
   7. spoons 8. baking
   9. dish 10. squares
   11. saucepun 12. mixture
B. a. 1. Take the ingredients out of the fridge.
      2. Mix eggs and milk together.
      3. Pour in flour and baking powder.
      4. Pour pancake batter onto a frying pan.
   b. 1. Buy a package of balloons.
      2. Take a balloon out of the package.
      3. Blow up the balloon.
      4. Twist the opening to make a knot.
C. (Individual writing)

5 Nunavut

A. 1. territory 2. North Pole
   3. six 4. night
   5. plants 6. cold
   (7. and 8. Suggested answers)
   7. clothes 8. skidoos
B. 1. Canada 2. months
   3. cold 4. bed
   5. school 6. dark
   7. night 8. north
   9. large 10. grow
   11. plants 12. near
C. (Suggested answers)
   2. can 3. ear 4. old

5. the 6. no 7. any
8. ants 9. row 10. here
11. dark 12. day 13. light
14. out 15. side
Challenge
   (Individual answers)
D. (Individual writing)

6 Word Fun

A. (Individual answers)
B.

C. 1. add 2. bear 3. blue
   4. buy 5. eye 6. read
   7. flower
D. (Individual writing)
E. (Individual writing and drawing)

7 What Makes a Fish a Fish?

A. (Suggested answers)
   1. bin ; pin 2. bet ; get
   3. bill ; fill 4. bail ; fail
   5. dish ; wish 6. bake ; cake
B. 1. oseans → oceans
   2. tales → tails
   3. scails → scales
   4. waive → wave
   5. eet → eat
   6. Their → There
   7. steams → streams
   8. aguariums → aquariums
C. 1. Fish live in ponds and oceans.
   2. Fish swim by moving their tails.
   3. All fish have backbones.
   4. Gills help fish to breathe.
   5. Scales protect the fish's skin.

6. Some fish make good pets.

D. (Individual writing)

Challenge

(Individual writing)

Progress Test 1

A.
1. box		2. cup	
3. sock		4. bat	
5. cake		6. milk	
7. goose		8. palm	
9. leaf		10. scales	
11. insect		12. gill	

B. (Suggested answers)

2. top	3. pot
4. art	5. ear
6. eat	7. wit
8. son	9. sum
10. old	11. and
12. is	13. ray
14. sea	15. our
16. cook	17. war
18. plan	

C.
1. Mike plays with his computer.
2. Amanda swims in her pool.
3. There are four books on the table.
4. The sun is hot today.
5. Caitlin has a pair of red shoes.
6. Bats look for food in the dark.

D.
1. skates	2. paints
3. driving	4. riding
5. plays	6. licking
7. watered	8. sucking
9. cut	10. danced

E.
1. sale → sail
2. plaid → played
3. maid → made
4. trayed → trade
5. eight → ate
6. male → mail
7. two → too
8. flour → flower

F. (Suggested answers)
1. maid ; paid ; raid	2. dot ; got ; jot
3. hour ; pour ; sour	4. pale ; sale ; tale
5. cap ; gap ; map	6. bin ; pin ; sin
7. bet ; get ; let	8. ball ; fall ; tall
9. bill ; fill ; hill	10. bake ; cake ; fake
11. fail ; jail ; sail	12. dear ; fear ; gear

8 Bat Facts

A. (Suggested answers)
1. bats	2. country
3. world	4. places
5. fruits	6. insects

B.

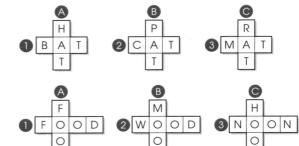

C. (Individual writing)

D. (Individual writing)

9 The Emperor Penguin

A.
1. penguin	2. Emperor
3. Antarctic	4. krill
5. hatches	6. patches
7. black	8. yellow
9. taller	10. grey / goes

B.
1. largest	2. penguin
3. feathers	4. ocean
5. shrimp	6. father

C.
1. The Emperor Penguin lives in Antarctica.
2. It lives near water, never on dry land.
3. Penguins get their food from the ocean.
4. Fish and krill are food for penguins.
5. The Emperor is the largest of penguins.
6. The mother penguin hunts for food.
7. The father Emperor hatches the egg.

D.
1. I love all kinds of candies. ~~Fish is not my favourite food.~~ My favourite candies are gummy bears.
2. I have a new bike. It is red and white. ~~The car goes in the garage.~~ My bike stays in the storage shed.
3. Amanda loves to swim in her pool. She asks her friends to come for a swim. ~~The flowers grow tall.~~ Her friends like to swim too.
4. Some of the best TV shows I like are really funny. They make me laugh and laugh. ~~My mom likes to dance.~~

10 Playing Soccer

A. (Individual writing)

B.

Column A	Column B
1. tall	ladybug
2. green	ball
3. tiny	knife
4. blue	girl
5. round	tree
6. sharp	grass
7. pretty	candy
8. sweet	sky
9. rainy	game
10. fun	day

C. (Colour the words.)
1. tiny   2. huge
3. twice   4. tall
5. a few   6. robbers
7. fast

D. 1. soccer   2. field
3. children   4. age
5. uniforms   6. coach
7. friendly   8. practise
9. games   10. fun

Challenge
(Individual writing)

11 Ladybugs

A. (Suggested answers)
1. best   2. hot
3. dug   4. hat
5. back   6. give
7. bill   8. come

B. 1. a bug that is red and black
2. an insect that eats plants and is eaten by ladybugs
3. They eat the inside of ladybugs.
4. someone or something that kills ladybugs
5. a spray to kill insects
6. a place where birds live
7. mess up
8. low green bushes
9. a bright colour
10. dots

C. 1. ladybug   2. insect
3. summer   4. useful

5. winter   6. disturb
7. because   8. lifetime

D. 1. Ladybugs are black and red. /
Ladybugs are red and black.
2. They live in flowers and shrubs. /
They live in shrubs and flowers.
3. They live in trees and houses in winter. /
They live in houses and trees in winter.
4. Ladybugs are useful because they eat insects.
5. Ladybugs are insects that eat aphides.
6. Ladybugs have some enemies.
7. Human beings are also the enemies of ladybugs.

12 The New Umbrella

A. (Suggested answers)
1. yell   2. hen   3. so
4. in   5. hat   6. old
7. sun   8. eat   9. ears
10. out   11. or   12. as

B.

e	r	t	y	a	j	m	r	y	u	d	e	m	v	t	y
c	n	k	i	g	r	n	o	e	f	i	S	e	d	e	w
t	i	u	m	b	r	e	l	l	a	e	c	l	o	f	g
w	a	n	E	y	e	w	o	l	y	m	o	d	e	r	n
p	l	i	g	a	d	m	n	o	w	a	t	f	a	r	d
h	S	o	q	r	b	o	t	w	i	r	l	d	E	o	r
l	a	z	s	q	u	i	b	r	h	i	a	e	x	p	m
d	l	o	u	w	b	q	u	v	o	p	n	m	s	q	y
w	h	a	n	d	l	e	r	m	E	f	d	b	e	u	o
y	n	i	b	w	u	w	i	i	g	r	n	a	s	x	u
e	d	t	u	r	e	a	l	l	y	w	e	d	r	j	E
a	m	t	r	u	m	b	p	w	p	t	d	w	i	o	n
r	a	i	n	s	d	p	r	o	t	e	c	t	o	y	b
s	k	m	u	d	e	a	b	s	e	m	b	i	v	f	w
y	n	e	a	t	r	w	a	e	k	i	u	t	a	S	b

C. 1. My new umbrella is colourful. /
My colourful umbrella is new.
2. My umbrella is not too big.
3. It is fun to twirl the umbrella.
4. The first umbrella was used in Egypt.
5. The umbrella protects me from the sun.
6. Umbrellas were used in Scotland in the 1800's.
7. I use my umbrellas in the rain.

D. 1. My mom bought me an umbrella. It was a present for my seventh birthday. It is red, blue, and yellow. It looks really neat. ~~My mom made me a huge birthday cake.~~
2. I have a new umbrella. It is colourful. ~~It was cloudy yesterday.~~ I can use it in the rain and also in the sun.

3. My neighbour, Jenny, has an umbrella hat. It is an umbrella but it is also a hat. She wears it on her head. ~~We often play together after school.~~ She looks cute in her umbrella hat.

E. (Individual drawing and writing)

13   Sam the Firefighter

A. 1. firefighter   2. works
   3. station   4. equipment
   5. friends   6. duty
   7. hours   8. hoses
   9. house   10. clean
  11. sometimes   12. overnight

B. 1. There were lots of bluejays in the garden. They were eating seeds and sitting on tree branches. ~~We had lunch there.~~
   2. Sunflowers can grow almost as tall as a one-storey house. ~~The apple is tasty.~~ Even the sunflower seeds are pretty big.
   3. William has a new red bike. He can ride it without training wheels. ~~His sister has a toothache.~~
   4. Jane liked the flowers. ~~She went to school.~~ She picked some flowers for her dad.
   5. Vincent ran all the way to the park. He played on the monkey bars. ~~William went shopping with his mom.~~
   6. There are seven days in every week. Sunday is the first day of the week. ~~I enjoyed the show.~~ Saturday is the last day.
   7. Our car was dirty. We went to the carwash yesterday. ~~There are little flies in the bushes.~~ Now the car is clean and shiny.

C. 1. eight   2. bare
   3. buy   4. sense
   5. wait   6. sum
   7. here   8. new
   9. flour   10. cell
  11. be   12. court

D. (Individual writing)

14   The Cactus

A. (Individual writing)
B. 1. dessert → desert
   2. shellow → shallow
   3. cactas → cactus
   4. peried → period

5. expends → expands
6. stord → stored
7. think → thick
8. ranefall → rainfall

C. 1. hot → cold
   2. much → little
   3. short → long
   4. slowly → quickly
   5. thin → thick
   6. shrinks → expands
   7. thick → shallow

D. (Individual writing)

15   Marineland

A. 1. Marineland is in Niagara Falls, Canada.
   2. There are sea animals there.
   3. There is so much fun in Marineland.
   4. Roller-coaster rides are very exciting.

B.

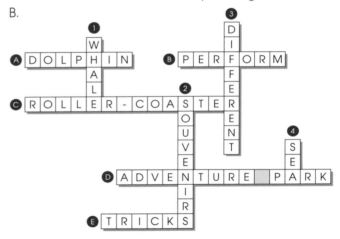

C. 1. Moon   2. Apple
   3. Red   4. I
   5. Nest   6. Easy
   7. Ladybug   8. Ant
   9. Night   10. Dog
   MARINELAND

D. (Individual writing)
Challenge
   (Individual drawing and writing)

Progress Test 2

A. 1. doll   2. books
   3. bike   4. cat
   5. dog   6. popsicles
   7. pillow   8. house

9. clown
10. plant
11. bed
12. car
13. glass
14. light
15. tree
16. cap
17. girl
18. firefighter
19. street
20. box
21. day
22. breakfast
23. road
24. whale

F. 1. trane → train
2. peeple → people
3. fiends → friends
4. seads → seeds
5. advanture → adventure
6. friut → fruit
7. petting → patting
8. glass → grass
9. Penquins → Penguins
10. feeld → field

B.

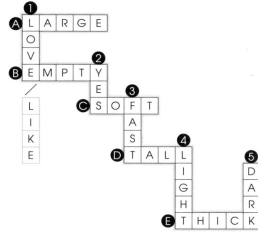

C. 1. My favourite candies are jujubes. /
Jujubes are my favourite candies.
2. Judy is my sister's good friend. /
My sister's good friend is Judy.
3. Ice cream is so good in summer.
4. Many people visit Toronto Zoo.
5. I like to go swimming.
6. We read a lot of books.
7. Firefighters work for many hours.
8. Dolphins are clever sea animals.

D. 1. large
2. small
3. quickly
4. one time
5. smart
6. pretty
7. much
8. kind

E. (Suggested answers)
1. best
2. up
3. pick
4. bead
5. new
6. stay
7. beat
8. deal
9. pour
10. brain
11. whale
12. turn
13. late
14. hand
15. drop
16. never
17. dare
18. treat
19. gill
20. aid
21. mug
22. live
23. full
24. sold

1. 1. clock   2. glue
   3. black   4. sled
   5. plus   6. flag

2.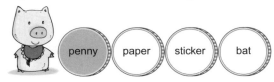

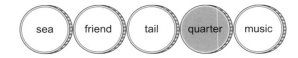
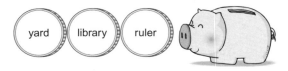

penny | paper | sticker | bat
boat | dime | toonie | nickel | lake
sea | friend | tail | quarter | music
bunny | jump | milk | loonie | ladder
yard | library | ruler

3.

s	b	l	i	f	e	b	e	l	t
u	a	q	c	k	v	s	o	p	o
n	m	n	s	g	d	u	e	a	w
g	p	b	d	o	j	n	w	i	e
l	m	h	r	c	s	h	e	l	l
a	k	c	t	e	a	w	a	z	s
s	a	n	d	o	l	s	j	t	p
s	e	a	g	u	l	l	t	y	a
e	x	r	l	e	n	v	a	l	d
s	w	i	m	s	u	i	t	e	e

4. 1. radio   2. dolphin
   3. fish   4. pen
   5. second

5. (Suggested answers)
   1. son   2. far
   3. ape   4. bed
   5. pal   6. hose

6.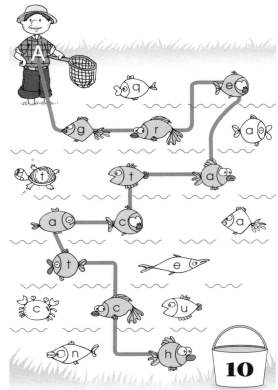

7.

¹M	O	U	S	E			³F		
I				G		⁴B	I	R	⁵D
L		⁶P	I	G			S		O
⁷K	⁸R			S			H		G
	A								
	⁹B	U	¹⁰N	N	Y			¹¹C	
	B		O					A	
	I		S		¹²W	I	N	G	S
¹³T	O	E	S					E	

8. 1. fawn   2. puppy
   3. duckling   4. cub
   5. piglet   6. calf

9.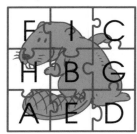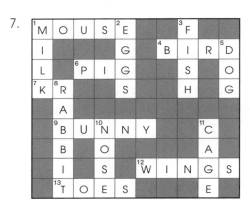

beaver   rat / mouse

10.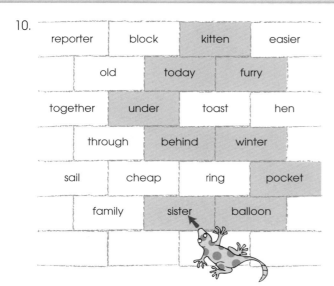

reporter	block	kitten	easier
	old	today	furry
together	under	toast	hen
	through	behind	winter
sail	cheap	ring	pocket
family	sister	balloon	

11. ink – pink ; dot – spot ; talk – walk ; boat – float ;
cake – bake ; swim – dim

12.

c	m	g	o	s	p	r	a	c	x	a	p
g	h	o	r	s	e	a	f	o	t	c	i
k	d	t	a	h	o	d	u	p	e	l	e
n	y	x	b	k	c	o	w	i	t	o	s
s	a	u	b	c	t	g	o	g	a	q	h
o	e	d	i	g	o	o	s	e	b	a	e
d	t	u	t	p	a	r	a	o	b	t	e
v	m	c	h	i	c	k	e	n	i	b	p
g	c	k	d	g	d	s	m	h	f	w	r
o	r	c	n	v	p	z	e	z	q	x	n
a	j	u	o	a	x	g	b	y	u	d	w
t	u	r	k	e	y	c	s	b	v	t	k

13.

14. 1. Monkey   2. Giraffe
    3. Gorilla   4. Elephant
    5. Panda   6. Lion

15.

	O	N	E		W	A	S	P	S
		E			N				T
M	O	S	Q	U	I	T	O		I
O		T			S				N
T							P		G
H		C	R	I	C	K	E	T	S
		R					S		
		A		B	E	E	T	L	E
		W		E			S		G
	F	L	I	E	S				G

16.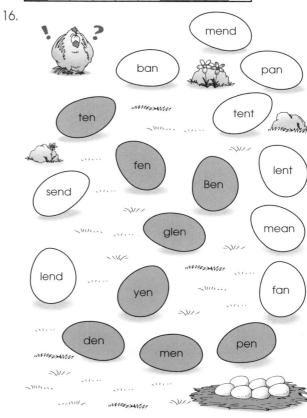

mend, ban, pan, ten, tent, fen, Ben, lent, send, glen, mean, lend, yen, fan, den, men, pen

17.

18. (Individual colouring)

c	p	k	g	s	f	r	e	l	a	p	h
f	i	q	x	m	o	w	h	i	t	e	n
h	n	b	p	c	u	b	l	y	v	k	i
d	k	a	o	w	g	r	e	e	n	o	t
b	g	t	r	n	c	o	j	l	w	x	f
l	m	e	a	y	m	w	b	l	u	e	r
a	i	p	n	d	g	n	h	o	a	s	d
c	n	u	g	r	q	i	t	w	l	z	j
k	s	r	e	d	k	z	c	o	q	b	v
o	j	a	v	e	p	u	r	p	l	e	m

19. My naughty dog hides his favourite bones under my bed.

20.

¹W	²A	T	E	R	M	E	L	³O	N
	P							R	
⁴P	E	A	⁵R		⁶E	A	T
	L		I			N	
	E		P			G	
	⁷P	E	E	L		E	
	E			⁸S		
	⁹A	P	R	I	C	O	T
	C			U		
	H		¹⁰R	E	D